SOMETHING

TO BE

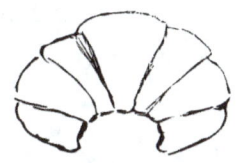

PROUD OF

A MEMOIR ON SMALL BUSINESS
AND THE BIGGER BUSINESS OF PURSUING ONE'S PASSION

MARTIN TIONGSON

First edition

Print Book ISBN: 979-8-9920136-0-3

eBook ISBN: 979-8-9920136-1-0

To My Mom.
For Everything.

Don't put all your eggs in one basket.
Don't count your chickens before they hatch.
A bird in the hand is worth two in the bush.

Contents

PROLOGUE

I RARELY SPEAK in absolutes. Most of the time, my answer is, "it depends." It depends on the set of factors, circumstances, and nuances of each unique situation. In that regard, there is no catch-all solution or course of action that applies to every situation. I don't feel comfortable giving an opinion on a matter that I don't know much about. I would need more information to form an opinion. I don't pretend to know the future. All I can do is relay the experiences I had, the decisions or actions that I took, and their respective outcomes.

I recognize that I am not an "ideas" person. I am an "operations" person who can implement and execute day in and day out. That is why I've mostly worked for companies or purchased existing businesses.

Recently, I took the time to be introspective and look back on my last fourteen years' worth of experiences working in small businesses: an Italian Gelateria, a Bagel Shop, and a French Bakery. I wanted to put pen to paper and write this book as a capstone to close that chapter of my life.

This is a collection of stories from my fourteen years in small business, both as an employee and employer. Each chapter of this book represents a different year from 2011 to 2024, including my experiences, takeaways, and everything in between.

Writing this book has been tedious and draining, but ultimately fulfilling. It has helped me untangle, uproot, and identify a cavalcade of emotions that have come out after sitting still in silence without the distractions of work. I hadn't been able to do that in a really long time until I started the writing process.

This is a memoir about small business and the bigger business of pursuing one's passions. I think the steps and actions I have taken stemmed from the simple desire to do something that I can be proud of. I think that is a common thread that we all aspire to—to be proud of something, whether in our personal life or professional career. To build something. Whether it gets torn down in the end or continues to live on without you, it remains with you—the doing it and having done it. To look at yourself and say, "I did it. I became it." There's no better feeling in the world.

CHAPTER 1

2011

IT ALL STARTED when I received an email for a job interview for a Gelato Shop in South Carolina. It was ten hours away from where I used to live in Miami. I did not apply or even know about this company. So many years later and I still don't know how they found out about me. I was relieved. For the last couple of months, I had sent out hundreds of job applications, and none of them had gotten off the ground. Then this one fell from the sky out of nowhere. A lucky break for once. Suffice to say, I desperately needed and wanted this job opportunity. I was asked to apply for the position of store operations manager. I didn't even have the experience for it. I had a corporate background as an associate and analyst.

I knew that I had to compensate for my shortcomings by setting myself apart from the other candidates. I had to bring something to the table that only I could bring. I searched for an arrow in my quiver. In school, I had won an award for a business plan I prepared, so I decided to create one for this company. Perfect. It would show that I was prepared and knew the small company beforehand, and it would offer tangible proof of my qualifications and abilities. I researched the company, market, and industry they were in. I packed for the trip and got in my car to go to the job interview. With me was a concise, thirty-page business plan and concept paper. It is always more persuasive to show rather than explain the initiative, thoughtfulness, and passion that you can offer an employer. I think any hiring manager would appreciate someone who will show the drive and willingness to go above and beyond. I also like to think that doing so makes it impossible for an employer to turn me down (or at least make them regret it if they did).

I showed up to my interview, where I met with the owners and key members of the leadership team. They expressed hesitation at my lack of relevant experience. In the end, however, they saw my potential and knew that it would outweigh my weakness. I received a job offer, which would be the beginning of my long journey in small business.

When looking back at the sequence of events that transpired in my professional career, I honestly didn't have a roadmap or a fixed destination in mind. One step just naturally led to the next one. I based my decisions on the logical next move, one after the other. It was a series of navigations, treading water and jumping at the right time. I consider work experience to be the most important thing when you start your own business, especially when it's in the same field. In that way, I'm not the best advocate for formal education (unless you pursue a career in a technical field). The lessons from this job had more applications in business and in life than the lessons I learned in school.

THE GELATO SHOP

The Gelato Shop was tucked away in a small commercial center which was designed to feel like a quaint village in the forest. The greenery was perfectly manicured and water fountains carefully maintained. At the same time, the giant pine trees surrounding the cluster of one-story structures evoked the natural growth of the woods. It was idyllic, pristine and picturesque. A strong sense of community permeated among the merchants with themed events and activities which were scheduled through the year.

The inside of the Gelato Shop reflected the whimsy and wonder that we sought to elicit from everyone who walked in our doors. The store had cheerful, peach-colored walls with lemon yellow accents and azure countertops. Pendant light lamps which matched the countertops warmly illuminated the space. Under the antique silver Milan ceiling tiles were stainless steel tables and chairs purposefully imported from Italy while depictions of famous landmarks served as the backdrop.

The piece de resistance was the gelato case or dipping cabinet in the center of the shop and visible from the outside. In it were pans of gelato in a rainbow of colors like art to be admired, appreciated and consumed, quite literally. We rotated among forty flavors of gelato and sorbetto. This excluded the seasonal flavors which customers looked forward to around the year. For fall, there were flavors like Pumpkin Spice, Cinnamon, Pumpkin Nutella Pie, Apple Pie and Coffee Cake. For winter, there were Winter Mint, Candy Cane, Bourbon Brown Butter Pecan, Grapefruit-Cranberry and Italian Eggnog.

LEARNING ON THE JOB

I soon learned how tough my first year in the Gelato Shop would be. Since I didn't have practical experience in store operations management, I found myself learning while on the job. I'm sure that my co-workers were frustrated with my steep learning curve. Something that was common sense to them seemed alien or unknown to me. I feel like I came close to being fired a number of times in that first year. During my first week, my car broke down, so I called out of work. I didn't know how big of a deal that was. In my mind, I prioritized fixing my car so that I would be able to get to work reliably and quickly in the future. However, how would the Gelato Shop open if no one was there to do it? That incident taught me to take a different approach. Find a ride to work and fix the car after the work day. For most companies, a new employee might be considered disposable at that stage, since they have not invested in their training. I am sure that it made a jarring second impression.

Another time, I was manning the store by myself. A restaurant across the street called to place a delivery. I closed the store, left a note on the door, and delivered the gelato. When I got back, my manager was there. She was furious. She told me never to close the store during hours of operation. Instead, call someone for help. Got it. After those incidents, I made sure to make up for my mistakes. I needed to learn as fast and work as hard as I could. I was committed to catching up, even just to reach the level where I needed to be. Most jobs are about being prepared, anticipating your manager's needs, and handing in your deliverables in line with their expectations and timeline.

I will admit that while the financial compensation left something to be desired, the lessons I learned in small business were priceless. They say when you get a job; it is either to earn or to learn. One is good. Both are better. The owner-president of the Gelato Shop was generous with teaching me everything about running her business. In that sense, I was training how to be an entrepreneur, as it covered all aspects of business, from day-to-day operations to accounting to inventory management to human resources to technology and everything in between.

In addition to routine work, I was also tasked with projects that had to be completed within a reasonable timeframe and budget. The ongoing project list included repairs, asset purchases, store improvements, and much more. These projects often started as ideas from the owners or us employees. Then they would get approved and assigned a person to carry them out.

One simple thing that resonated with me was that bills had to be paid just on time—not early so as to preserve cash flow, but not late either so as to incur late fees. I have taken this way of approaching bills to my own business as well as my personal finances. The owner of the Gelato Shop was incensed if bills were paid late, particularly if late fees were incurred. She taught me diligence, mindfulness, and organization when it came to bills payable. I don't think I've ever paid a bill late since.

She also believed in awards and recognition as a tool for marketing. To this end, we participated in contests, competitions, fundraisers, and charitable events. Besides the intended purpose of these events, it kept the company's name current and on top of people's minds.

My last important takeaway from this job was related to documentation. Everything needs to be documented. You never know if you might need to circle back to it in the future. The act of documentation will save you a lot of grief, headaches, and possibly even money. It might even prevent conflicts and legal bills in your future.

CHAPTER 2

2012

FOR A SMALL BUSINESS, the Gelato Shop I worked in had a lot of components and pieces that made up the whole. I was hired to be the manager of their headquarters, which was also called its corporate store. This location had two prongs. The first was the retail side, which included walk-in customers and catering orders. The second was the wholesale side, where we sold gelato to local businesses like hotels, resorts, golf clubs, and restaurants. We also had a portable cart for special occasions such as birthdays, weddings, and promotional events like art shows, bridal shows, fairs, tournaments, conferences, and exhibits.

Besides the corporate store, there were the licensee stores and airport stores. The licensee stores were operated by signed licensees of the business, often private individuals or groups who wanted to start their own business but needed a structure and a guiding hand. (Licensees are similar to franchisees, but the license model's legal structure is less restrictive or rigid than a franchise model.) The airport stores were operated by the respective airport concessions, which had a contract with the Gelato Shop. The licensees and airports carried the Gelato Shop's name and product. In turn, the Gelato Shop made money by selling the product to these entities at a profit.

I didn't know it at the time, but working at the Gelato Shop proved to be a valuable and necessary learning experience. It became like a laboratory (with sixty flavors) where I could conduct trial and error experiments and hone the abilities and skills I needed for small business.

The goal of any business is to make a profit. The Gelato Shop broke it down for me into two simple concepts that resonated with me and became my guidepost in all the years since: increase sales or lower costs. Whenever profits or profit margins started to decline, I would ask myself if there were ways to accomplish either. I would make sure that the store had sufficient inventory in order to avoid stock outs. I would upsell to customers and facilitate return visits. I would renegotiate service agreements, shop around for more cost-effective options, cut unnecessary costs and reduce waste.

A typical day would entail opening and setting up the shop, serving customers until the staff was scheduled to come in, being their backup when it got busy, cleaning, organizing, restocking, going to the bank to deposit the previous day's cash sales and get change, placing orders with vendors, paying vendor bills, cold calling wholesale customers, creating customer invoices, delivering gelato to wholesale customers, collecting payments, making gelato cakes, running to the grocery store for supplies like cake boxes, clearing and closing the store, and bookkeeping. At night, I would work on my reports for the monthly meetings and work on special projects on our project list. Over time, I got more adept and was able to pack in more and more things in a single day.

I also educated customers on the difference between gelato and ice cream. Gelato was made with more milk and natural ingredients but less fat content. It was stored and served at a higher temperature than ice cream which attributed its silkier mouthfeel. It was also churned more slowly which made it denser and less aerated than ice cream.

VARIANCE

Portion control is a significant issue for any gelato or ice cream shop where the product is scooped by the servers. Over-scooping can pose a serious problem for owners because it can significantly alter cost of goods. It can really add up in a surprisingly big way. Scoop size had to be continuously emphasized and repeated to staff so that they understood why it was so important.

The owner of the Gelato Shop suspected that employees were over-scooping, but we didn't have any meaningful or quantitative data to determine just how much gelato was being lost on a recurring basis. She tasked me to find out.

My first objective was monitoring. I did this by creating a variance report where I compared standard usage versus actual usage of product. The standard usage was determined through a motion study, which determined that a pan of gelato can yield thirty standard-sized scoops. Monthly standard usage was determined by obtaining the monthly sales report from the point of sale system. From there, the standard number of pans was back calculated from how many scoops were sold within that timeframe.

On the other hand, monthly actual usage was determined by calculating the actual number of pans of gelato that was used within the same timeframe. Basically, the equation was number of pans at the start of the month plus number of pans delivered minus number of pans left at the end of the month.

The difference between the actual number of pans used (which was always larger) and the standard number of pans yielded the variance, which could be attributed to all of the following: handling, sampling, over-scooping, transferring to new containers, fluffing, cleaning, refilling, and recording mistakes. I analyzed each of these activities and ways to reduce product loss. Still, over-scooping was known to be the biggest culprit.

We established an acceptable variance rate at 4%. Above that would be deemed avoidable product waste. Now that we had quantitative data, there had to be a meaningful way to actually effect change, which was the whole point of the endeavor.

After monitoring, my second objective was to make improvements that would result in a reduction in the monthly variance rate. I did this by establishing an employee incentive program where staff would get certain bonuses if they reached different variance rates that were within the acceptable threshold.

It took a few months to continuously hone the variance report and employee incentive program, but they proved to be very useful tools for the company. We were able to keep track and improve cost of goods by reducing avoidable product waste. Of course, there were still ups and downs from month to month, but the general trajectory was positive.

Noticeably, the variance rate tended to go up when more gelato was sold. The logical explanation was that scoopers tended to forget and over-scoop when it got really busy. Their priority shifted to speed and not accuracy of the correct portion size.

WHOLESALES

The Gelato Shop gave me my first taste in wholesales as a salesperson. It was nerve-wracking because I'm a natural introvert. The prospect of meeting and engaging with new people was a scary concept for me. I wasn't charismatic or personable in the way that I thought a salesperson needed to be.

I met with chefs and procurement managers in restaurants and hotels around town in order to sell them gelato. They could put the gelato on their dessert menu or use it as a component in their own dessert recipes. Like with all things, repeated exposure and practice eased my anxiety and built my confidence. I was actually able to go out and get people to buy something from me! Of course, it helped that I had a wonderful product to sell. I developed my own style that naturally worked for me as a salesperson.

I was cordial and professional to my customers. More importantly, I was consistent and reliable. Wholesale customers had a job to do as well, so they wanted to keep working with a good supplier. I would do my rounds. I visited regular and lapsed customers. I made sales calls to leads or potential customers in the hope of activating them as accounts. The key to sales was repetition and regular follow-up. The chefs were often busy, so it was about catching them at the right time. I took notes, studied them, and remembered them. In that way, I had a profile for each lead or customer I could refer to when preparing for future visits. I collated all of the information in a dashboard, where I tracked my weekly progress in terms of productivity (number of calls, visits, and hours) and effectiveness (lead acquisition, account retention, customer turnover).

Because we had a lean team, I handled delivery and payment collection as well. I also updated marketing materials and ran promotions like a discount and loyalty program, a trigger campaign, and a rewards program for the recommendation and referral of potential customers.

The marketing materials were a vital tool for sales. They sold the vision to potential customers through tangible documents like pricing and gross profit analysis, product recommendations and recipes, a flavor list, benchmarking studies for pricing and taste, and customer reviews.

I found my own way as a salesperson, and I felt so proud that I was able to outdo my performance every year. I increased sales by 50% each year. All of these activities allowed me to have a big-picture overview of sales.

SUPPLY CHAIN

If that weren't enough, the Gelato Shop was also my first

exposure to logistics, warehousing, and distribution, which are equally vital components of business. I updated and disseminated product-receiving procedures to warehouses and freight companies. This was to make sure quality standards were upheld and controlled at every single step of the transportation and storage of gelato. Processes included taking and monitoring temperature, inspecting for any visible damages or defects, and only accepting product in good condition. We also inspected and audited products, received and processed customer complaints, and brought any complaints to the attention of the responsible partner for resolution.

I tried to separate myself from the complaints and told myself they were things that needed to get done. It was sometimes difficult because the party found responsible (co-packer, warehouse, freight) would not process the complaints easily, which made sense, as issuing large credits or refunds ate away at their own profit. When one pan of gelato was damaged, you could expect there to be more damaged pans in the pallet. That's why documentation like formal correspondences and pictures were so important.

Small business is like a burning fire that needs to be tended to and fed kindling to keep alive. Yet it is intentional and so needs to be tamed. It can't grow too large or too quick or it will be out of control. The natural state of small business is entropy. There were always wildfires to put out, which prepared me well for the future.

CHAPTER 3

2013

I STARTED AS THE STORE MANAGER at the Gelato Shop. Once I got a handle on a task that I was assigned, I would be given more and more responsibilities, until I was involved in all aspects of the business.

Every day was different. There were so many things to do, but I loved every part of it. I truly poured myself into this job. I was assigned important and pivotal projects in the company's growth plans, like the creation and occasional revisions of materials like playbooks, strategic plans, and operations and training manuals. However, my favorite part of the job was just fluffing or swirling the gelato at night. I could just shut off my brain, let my hands work, and be rewarded with intricately swooped and swirled stacks of creamy goodness. We displayed them like towers in the gelato case to be admired and complimented by customers. I looked forward to the flavors that would signal each season, like pumpkin spice for fall and spumoni for winter.

Each business owner has their own definition of success, whether it's steady income or wealth creation. It can be the ease of being your own boss or vanity to put a shine on your name. For the Gelato Shop, it was name and brand recognition through expansive growth, reach, and acclaim. No expense was spared in pursuing different growth opportunities, whichever direction or form it took.

We sent samples to people who could potentially offer us a way in to different opportunities like TV shows. Perhaps there were too many balls in the air. In my opinion, we didn't close all that many deals considering how much effort, money, and time was spent on growth plans. With small business, a lot of work goes on behind closed doors, and perceptions can often be deceiving. You can't tell from the outside which company is making money and which company is not. It's only when you look at their financial statements that you will know.

A complexity that this business had was cash flow. We had a single co-packer that supplied our gelato, yet we had a number of airport and licensee customers that bought the gelato from us—meaning that the amounts on outgoing payments were much more significant than those on incoming payments. This substantially affected the business bank account's balance at any given time. Sometimes there wouldn't be enough funds to send out the checks to the co-packer. We would need to draw funds from the line of credit or the loan. So there was a constant back-and-forth between paying and drawing from the line of credit. This is not something you would normally witness with a traditional retail store location where money from sales are immediate and cash-based, at most delayed by a day because of credit card processing.

BUDGET PLANNING

The purpose of a budget is to set an intention. What are the company's goals and benchmarks for the coming fiscal year? What special projects are planned and what is their projected spend? Budget setting becomes more important as the company gets bigger; more complex and harder to control.

My first job after I graduated from college was in corporate planning in a multinational manufacturing and distribution company of branded food products. The most definitive skill I transferred from my old job to the Gelato Shop was helping management formalize a line-by-line item budget for the fiscal year and updating those forecasts every month or quarter.

With any business, the goal is to remain as close as possible to the budget that was approved by management before the fiscal year. At the same time, flexibility to deviate from the budget needs to be allowed. Mitigating circumstances are likely to arise throughout the year, much like the sun rises and sets. Top management also has the ability to reallocate budgets to higher priority activities or make changes to the rest of the budget, as resources and other factors might change as well.

A company doesn't exist in a vacuum, so comparing the budget to actual figures can help explain to management why any goals have not been met or numbers exceeded. Hard numbers need to be coupled with qualitative information to paint a full story. For example: What were the reasons why sales numbers were exceeded, and how can we keep doing it? Or, what were the reasons why sales were not met, and what can we learn from it? It's all about accountability and whether those reasons are deemed acceptable or necessary by the owners or officers of the organization. It's also good practice to include copious notes to explain budget divergences and ensure that lessons are learned from mistakes.

In the Gelato Shop, we broke down the budget into months, categories, and locations. Forecasts were updated every quarter by replacing the budgeted monthly P&L (profit and loss) by the actual monthly P&L. Everything was detailed enough to allow some meaningful interpretation, however, not too detailed so as to cause analysis paralysis or make the exercise futile.

ORDER TO CASH MANAGEMENT

One important responsibility I took over from my manager was the complete order-to-cash management between the gelato company, its licensee customers, and its co-packer. Licensee customers would order from us. In turn we would either schedule a delivery from one of our warehouses or order product from our co-packer to be shipped directly to the licensee customer. The co-packer was the supplier that produced the Gelato Shop's branded gelato using proprietary recipes.

I was very nervous when I took over, since it was such a critical responsibility. Any mistakes or oversight would have been visible to so many stakeholders, including customers, warehouses, the supplier, and my managers. I surprised myself in the end. I found out how good I was at this job. By the time it was given to me, I was more than ready. I loved it because it entailed organization, planning, attention to detail and schedules, mindfulness, and timing. I personally thought that I did a fantastic job because I made sure we were well-stocked at all times. I anticipated need, so we never ran out of inventory. I proactively reached out to customers if they needed to place an order before cut-off times. Consequently, we always delivered our customers' orders on time. At the same time, I had to consider inventory space and cash in the bank, which were both limited and meant that I couldn't order too much or too far in advance.

This responsibility also included receiving payments from customers and making payments to the supplier. The two key words were: on time. I surprised myself again with how good of a job I did. I reduced the aging time of bills from customers in a substantial way. I did this by staying on top of collecting bills and making sure that due dates were communicated and sometimes reiterated well in advance. I also think I was able to establish good relationships with customers because I facilitated a smooth and seamless process from order to delivery. Having satisfied customers carried over to their payments being made on time. In turn, this enabled the Gelato Shop to pay our supplier just on time—not too early as a consideration to cash flow, but not late as to incur late charges.

It might not have been the most sophisticated system, but the way I went about everything was to put together a simple document that contained the order-to-cash process flowchart, supply chain network (customers, warehouses, and suppliers), contact persons and information, customer payment methods, and a weekly and monthly schedule that specified when to send email reminders, email confirmations, order cut-off times, and delivery days. The document became the bible that I referred to every day. The last steps were religiously entering everything (purchase orders – sales orders – invoices – payments) into the bookkeeping software and an Excel database to help keep track of everything and make sure nothing was missed.

SECURITY POLICY

Another important aspect of small business is having guidelines in place in order to protect people, materials, and data against potential risks, threats, and situations that could compromise their safety and integrity. I thought about these quite a lot, so I assembled a consolidated security policy as a readily available reference.

People security meant safety precautions and policies for employees, customers, and vendors. This comprised information on the store's security system, emergency protocols, background screening for hiring, and drug-free workplace policy. Workers' compensation and the liability-insurance policy were also included, as well as the nutrition and allergen handbook, 911 and CPR training, mopping policy, and first-aid list.

Materials security meant safety precautions and policies for food, cash, and store assets. Food safety comprised information on the annual health inspection, food protection manager certification, and sanitation standards. Cash security and store assets security comprised cash-handling guidelines, training and maintenance of store equipment, emergency and evacuation plans, and disaster, hurricane, and flood-awareness planning.

Data security meant safety precautions and policies for credit card, company, and proprietary data. This comprised the data security handbook, which aimed to reduce the risk from hackers. Confidential and proprietary information agreements were signed by all employees. Confidential and critical data was kept on a restricted, need-to-know basis. The storage and access of physical and digital files were safeguarded in compliance with data-safety regulations. Measures were in place to respond in case of data compromise or a security breach.

Contrary to common belief—and purely in terms of security—small business is anything but simple. My years working in the Gelato Shop proved to be very busy and interesting. All I remember was work and sleep, but you have to make sacrifices to do what you want to do.

CHAPTER 4
2014

WHAT WAS THE LAST STRAW that made me decide to leave? We always had a very lean team. Besides the two owners, there were three full-time employees including myself. By this time, the two long-term employees had left in short succession. There was a flux of replacements coming in and going out. They didn't stick around very long. There was a disconnect between the two owners and me. They had very high standards for the staff, and they turned to me to terminate members who were not performing to their expectations.

The directive was to tighten the belt and cut back on shifts to save money. However, the store was still so busy during the summer that I couldn't realistically find a way of doing it without impacting the other employees or affecting our usual level of customer service. The store made ten times more in its busiest month than on its slowest month. Consequently, this made seasonal staffing a feature of the business and not a bug in the system.

In the middle of a busy shift one night, one of the owners came into the shop and took me aside. Due to the directive to cut back on hours, he told me to send home one of the staff and terminate her effective immediately, as she was the newest customer service associate. It was a long time ago now, but I remember how that moment made me feel. I was infuriated. I was busting my chops, having worked so hard for so long, and it was still not good enough. I recognize in this moment that I was highly emotional. I imagined being in the employee's shoes. I would not want to be treated that way if I were the staff member; asked to go home in the middle of a shift and to only be compensated for the hour that you were there. I talked to her to convey what I had been told, apologized for the inconvenience, and asked her to leave. I pulled my own money from my pocket and compensated her for the full night's shift.

After that, the owner's niece and nephew came to work for the Gelato Shop. The difference in how they were treated (and paid) compared to the other employees, including myself, was palpable. It also caused resentment in my co-workers, who were very close to the owners and had once seemed like their own family. I vowed never to employ family members if I had my own business. I wouldn't want my employees to feel the way I felt then.

TECHNOLOGY

The major project for that year was an ambitious and expensive system migration from Quickbooks, which is relatively simple bookkeeping software, to Netsuite. This change was directed by the owner in order to have a robust, comprehensive and integrated inventory planning and order-to-cash management system. She spared no expense, as we not only had to pay for the subscription, but we also needed to engage with consultants, trainers, and IT specialists to get it up and running. This was a considerable strain on the employees. With money already tight, I didn't think it a wise decision to allocate precious resources to this particular project. It could have been a beneficial improvement on the current system, but it was adopted too early and too soon.

I was running on fumes. My emotions (and blood pressure) also ran high without my knowing. In one instance, I was working alone in the office when the phone rang. The person on the other end of the line said that they were calling from the electric company. They had not received our check and were going to cut the store's power. I was in charge of paying the bills, and I was sure that I had mailed that month's check. I relayed my response to the person I was speaking with. He said in a matter-of-fact tone that they had not received payment, so I needed to send it right away. I started to doubt myself. Did I in fact mail that month's check, or did I forget? It was going to be my fault if we lost power. I was already under so much pressure. I begged and asked the person what I could do. He said a check would arrive too late, so he gave me instructions to go to the convenience store and purchase a gift card. Then, I would give him the gift card's code for the payment. I was in such a state of duress that it did not even click how bizarre and unusual his request was. I was going to do it. The pieces only came together when I walked out the door. I called my manager and confirmed that it was a scam. I called the person back and just told him shame on him for preying on innocent people. I decided then and there to always make a point of not making decisions under pressure and on the spot. Always assess first and sleep on it overnight if possible.

QUITTING

Another reason why I resigned was that we employees didn't receive bonuses that year. Previously, we had gotten annual and special bonuses. Having worked so hard and given so much of myself to the company, it felt hurtful not to be rewarded for it. Now, several years later, I understand the owners' position better. If a company is not very profitable, it can't afford to be too generous to their employees.

I submitted my resignation; twice actually. The owner convinced me to stay after the first one. Shortly after that, I sent in my final resignation. Once an employee becomes disengaged, it's improbable they will stick around much longer.

There were good times and good memories along with the bad. Although my last months there were bad, they don't define my overall experience at the Gelato Shop. My employers focused on employee enrichment by having us attend classes, seminars, and workshops. I got a couple of certificates from some courses I took that the business paid for. We participated in teambuilding exercises and activities. All in all, it was a positive and enriching experience. I look back at that time very fondly, and I still think very highly of my employers.

I loved the place that I lived and worked. It was a breath-taking resort town, and I lived on the water. On summer nights, I would sit on my balcony and watch the fireworks lighting up the sky. Winters were sleepy; you could hibernate in your bed and recuperate for a season. I would jump back there in a heartbeat. My only regret was not buying my apartment (not that I had the money, mind you).

The food was fresh and tasty. I miss my Piggly Wiggly (which is a supermarket if you don't know what a Piggly Wiggly is). I miss the boats docked on the marina. I miss the feeling of being content in your own company and not worrying about the future. I even miss the days and nights of setting up and dismantling the gelato cart, and of being the invisible, background figure when I had to scoop gelato at onsite events.

A SURPRISE AROUND THE CORNER

I didn't know what the next step was going to be, but staying at the Gelato Shop was untenable. In my last week, I decided to attend a roundtable event at the local chamber of commerce. That one hour meeting turned out to be an inflection point and changed the course of my life. The topic was entrepreneurship. It gave me the first tools for small business ownership through purchase of an existing business. It provided information on resources like a couple of how-to books that would become my guideposts. I already knew how to run a business, and now I knew how to get it started and set things in motion.

"How To Buy A Good Business At A Great Price: Your Roadmap To Success" by Richard Parker became my bible.

Ed Pendarvis' "Guide To Buying A Small Business" was a fantastic book and companion piece. The local Small Business Development Center was a treasure trove of information and proved to be a supportive network in getting started.

All people who go into business do it to be successful, but everyone's definition and version of success is different. For some people, success means multi-generational wealth from an entrepreneurial empire. For others, it simply means a steady income without the burdens and stress of growth and change. Success might not even be financial. It can be to add prestige to your name or build your credibility and reputation. Your driving force could be competition; to race to become an industry leader among your peers. Make sure that what you are doing is aligned with whatever definition of success you have, and be cognizant that other people's version of success might not be the same as yours.

In my opinion, personal traits don't make a person successful. It is the alignment or compatibility of your personal traits with your chosen profession that will determine whether you will be successful or not. For example, creativity is important in an artistic field but possibly not so much if your job is in operations management. On the other hand, consistency and timeliness are crucial in operations but not necessarily in the arts.

CHAPTER 5

2015

I WAS VERY CONFIDENT prior to starting my own business. I knew that I could do it because I was able to run another person's business. It was just a matter of applying that to my own venture. I would recommend that anyone gain employment experience first before owning a business in order to assess whether the idea in your mind matches the reality. Often, I find that people romanticize entrepreneurship and self-employment, but it is very different in real life, as it presents its own unique set of challenges. It is toil and grind.

Armed with some small business experience, knowledge, and seed money, I forged ahead towards small business ownership. I sought to buy a small store with a proven track record to operate and manage. From the chamber roundtable I had attended, I knew where to look for listings. The business had to be the right size to fit my budget. It also had to be something I could pick up easily and transfer my existing skills to. I am an analytical person, so profit potential was the most crucial factor to look for in a business. This can be assessed through due diligence, investigating, and cross-checking all aspects of a business.

Looking for a good business to buy is like looking for a needle in a haystack of fraudulent, failing, or unsustainable businesses. You have to sift through all of the chaff and separate the wheat. When I am given information verbally or in writing, I always consider the motive, intention, and agenda. Don't take anything at face value in business or in life.

Personally, I believe that the most critical numbers to look for when evaluating a business is revenue or sales. This information is easy to verify by matching and analyzing unaudited financial statements, monthly sales tax returns, bank account statements, and credit card merchant service statements (along with K-1s). Climbing sales are an excellent indicator of growth and profit potential. Sales volume determines whether a business can bring in sufficient funds to offset direct costs. There is typically a sales volume threshold a business has to reach in order to be profitable. Other numbers like operating expenses can be controlled, prioritized, or improved on. Sales show if the business has a product that people will pay money for, which is the foundational aspect of a for-profit business.

I tend to pay less attention to the bottom-line net income. This number is less easily verifiable. For me, it is acceptable if a seller doesn't provide the buyer with their annual tax returns. With a sole or partner proprietorship or an LLC, the business income tax often feeds into their personal income tax returns' Schedule C. The Schedule C is also audited by their CPA. In my experience, it doesn't paint a clear, concise, or accurate picture of the business, since its purpose of tax minimization is contrary to the buyer's purpose of evaluating its viability.

There are some simple ratios that can help identify whether a business can be profitable. For a retail store, the ideal percentage of rent to sales is 10-15%, and no more than that. Higher than that sweet spot signals that profitability will be more difficult to achieve. I don't rely on cost of goods or labor as much, as it depends on the nature of the particular business. For example, businesses that make everything from scratch are more labor intensive. Businesses that procure finished or close to finished goods from a co-packer or manufacturer are more cost of goods intensive. Those aspects can be played with later on through active owner involvement, negotiation, shopping better prices, streamlining operations, or improving efficiency.

At this point, I put together a timeline to purchase a business. I didn't have ties to where I was living, so I was open to relocating, depending on where the opportunity would arise. I looked at a few businesses up for sale in Los Angeles, San Francisco, Portland, and Seattle. These were the places I thought I'd like to live in. I browsed business listings, contacted sellers' brokers, received business prospectuses, conducted onsite visits, and arranged meetings with the owners. I was also looking for a CPA, a business attorney and an immigration attorney. (I had not immigrated at this time.) I crossed off gelato shops from my list of prospective businesses. In my experience, they were a highly temperamental product, literally. You have to constantly monitor them to make sure they are in the right temperature zone. Very big problems arise when coolers don't work how they're supposed to, and it's more common than you might think. My criterion was: I just wanted something that you can make and not worry too much about afterwards.

The first business I saw was a high-traffic sandwich shop on Embarcadero Drive in San Francisco. It was centrally located in a bustling financial district, with its primary business coming from nearby office workers during the workweek.

I was very impressed. Based on first impression, it was a fast-paced, money-making business. I met with the owner, but they were not flexible with the asking price, which was a little steep for me. In the end, purchasing the sandwich shop would max out my cash on hand. This was not a viable option because when buying a business, there are still additional costs after the purchase price, such as closing costs, rent deposit, starting working capital, and reserves for any repairs or replacements that might need to be done after the sale. It was a good business on the surface, but it wasn't compatible with my financial situation. It was too risky. This would be my only shot, and there would be no safety net if I failed. As sad as I was, it wasn't right for me. I had to move on to the next opportunity.

I drove from Los Angeles to Seattle, visiting my friend and former co-worker in Portland along the way. I saw a tea shop with two locations in Big Bear and Lake Arrowhead, a pastry shop in Murphys, a pie shop in Portland and a café on Mercer Island. I loved those short few weeks because it was an adventure. I was nervous at the same time because time was ticking and money was flowing out. I knew my decision would have a substantial impact for who knows how many years to come—or possibly the rest of my life. I was not wrong in this sentiment. I was singular in my focus.

The last business on my itinerary was a Japanese bakery in Seattle. It was perfect on paper. They sold baked goods using classical French techniques with Japanese flavors. They reported good earnings, and they had multiple income streams from walk-in and wholesale customers. I personally loved how their products tasted, and based on feedback and reviews, their customers agreed with me. Very promising. I met with the seller's broker, who then introduced me to the owner, founder, and namesake of the bakery.

I was satisfied with the information I had been given in the short prospectus and during my initial meeting with the owner. The business was the right size, and the purchase price was more suited for my budget. I signed the purchase and sale agreement (PSA), which outlined the terms and conditions of the sale and purchase of the business.

After the PSA was signed by both parties, the feasibility period followed. This typically lasts thirty days or some other agreed-upon timeframe. This is the time when the buyer can conduct their due diligence and a more thorough inspection of all aspects of the business in order to determine its feasibility. Having prepared and researched beforehand, I set off to do just that. I had so much confidence back then. The confidence compensated for my lack of experience. I'm not sure if I could do it all over again now. I got more conservative and careful with age, like most people.

I was methodical and detailed with my list of questions and materials I requested from the seller. The seller was very cooperative, responsive, and timely with submitting the documents I requested. I found him congenial and professional in our one-on-one meetings. We saw eye-to-eye on a lot of things. I was most hesitant about not having pastry experience, but he assured me that he would be able to train me and that I could replicate the products that the bakery was renowned for. After the sale, his plan was to move to La Conner, where he would open a high-end restaurant to fulfill his potential, as he was not only a pastry chef but a gifted culinary genius as well.

I engaged the services of a business attorney for this deal as recommended in my research. This was also my first experience buying a business, so I erred on the side of caution. I formalized my legal entity's operating agreement with the help of the business attorney. She was good at her job but very expensive, of course. Attorneys are tricky. They can be a lifesaver, but they can also be a fast drain on your resources, so you only engage them if you need to. On the other hand, you want a long-term relationship with your CPA year after year.

Everything looked good so far. The lease reassignment was reviewed by the business attorney and approved by the landlord. All that was left was closing—until a small snag hit. The operating agreement revealed that there were a few members in the LLC. The majority stakeholder was the active owner, and the rest were silent partners, probably his financiers. We discovered later on in the process that one of the partners did not want to sign off on the sale. My thinking was that this owner was receiving regular passive income from the store and did not want to give that up. The other possibility was that there might have been a falling out among owners, and the relationship had become acrimonious. The active owner I was speaking to assured me that it would not be an issue in the future.

Falling back on my experience at the Gelato Shop working under a very litigious owner, I just could not bring myself to take that risk and sign the deal only to possibly lose everything on a legal technicality. I was planning not only to buy the business, but grow and invest in it. The majority owner of the Japanese bakery came back to the table and offered a discount on the sale just to close it. He also invested his own time, energy, and money on this deal as the seller. However, having all of the members on the operating agreement sign the sale was a hard condition for me. It was not meant to be, and the deal did not close. It was unfortunate because I believed in the Japanese bakery's high growth and expansion potential. I regret how it ended with the owner of the Japanese bakery and the relationship I could have had with him. He was someone who I wanted to model myself after and whose trajectory I wanted to emulate. He could have been such an amazing mentor to have. Sadly, it was not meant to be.

Much later, I found out that the owner's employee ended up buying the bakery. I have had several experiences, directly and indirectly, of bakers buying the bakery that they worked in. So if you find yourself in a similar situation, remember that pretty much all bakers want to own their own bakery. This experience would haunt me later on.

While this deal was falling apart, a new listing popped up for a Bagel Store in the suburban area of a small city near Seattle. It sold sandwiches and coffee. I started investigating it as a back-up in case the deal with the Japanese bakery fell apart. As it turned out, it was not an exercise in futility.

The sellers of the Bagel Store were also its first owners. They had been in operation for less than two years. Right away, I asked about the ownership structure so I wouldn't run into the same problem I had with the Japanese bakery. There were three owners. The first owner was the active partner, who was involved in the day-to-day operations. The second owner was the financier and silent partner. The third owner was the owner of a bagel factory that was a separate legal entity. The factory was the Bagel Store's main supplier of bagels. It shipped the product to the store in the form of pucks—raw, pre-formed dough. Finishing touches and garnishes were done in the store every morning, before proofing and steam baking the bagels. This made the morning baking process relatively fast and easy, around ninety minutes to three hours, depending on the day of the week.

The vision of the original owners was to have a retail location in every city, and this store would be their pilot location. The problem they didn't foresee was that the active owner worked in a different industry and did not have food experience. Enthusiasm and excitement can carry you for a while, but it wanes. Until you are in the trenches, you truly won't know if you'll be able to sustain your ability in that line of work. The owner-operator also had a hard time working with bacon because of his religion. This was a big problem, as you can't have a bagel store without breakfast sandwiches, and you can't have breakfast sandwiches without bacon. The previous owner bought uncooked bacon and cooked it in the store's oven. This was a lot of work and cleaning, given the amount of bacon the store went through. It was messy, greasy, tedious, and cumbersome. (One of the first things I did when I came in was to switch to pre-cooked bacon. It was a little more expensive but so worth it. There was no pushback from customers whatsoever.)

My advice is always to work in food service before starting big and investing a lot of your own energy, money, and time. The picture in your head might not match with the reality of the daily grind. A lot of the time, people who have worked and built a career in a corporate setting romanticize the idea of working in a simple business, which it is often anything but.

After a couple of years, the active owner of the Bagel Store realized that it was not for him, so the other owners' decision was to dissolve the partnership and liquidate the asset. I asked if all three owners would sign on the sale. They said yes and that it would not be an issue.

I offered to buy the business at their asking price, although I knew it was inflated. I would be paying a premium over the present value of the business. There were several factors at play in my decision to not push back. First, I wanted to make sure that the owners would not entertain any other offers. Because of the last missed opportunity, I was depleting my funds fast. I could not afford to lose this deal. Second, I was going to have an ongoing relationship with the third owner as a main supplier, so I wanted to start on a positive note and make a good first impression. I was banking on the fact that this gesture would translate into goodwill and that he would be a good supplier to us. I learned from the Gelato Shop that a good supplier relationship is crucial to succeed in business. Along with this, I had him sign a supplier agreement as part of the closing documents to ensure that the price of the product would remain the same for three years. Third, I needed them to provide me with very detailed documentation and work on my timeline. Besides conducting my due diligence, I still had to secure my US visa. My strategy was for the long term. I sowed and planted seeds that I hoped to reap in the future. (As an aside, buyers who already failed a closing make for easier buyers.)

It was a very stressful time but rewarding by the same token. I felt like I was buying two businesses at the same time because of the business aspect and the immigration aspect. A lot of coordination and moving parts were involved. I needed to plan out everything and make the process as seamless as possible without wasting a lot of downtime. I was very proud of myself. The turnaround time was as expected. I lined up everything and knocked everything down. The Bagel Store was turnkey, so we were able to start operations the day after closing.

In the end, I secured the business. We closed and signed at the silent partner's office in his tower in downtown Seattle. He was apparently a very big deal according to the other owners. It was a very proud day; my first day as a business owner – July 20.

THE BAGEL STORE

The Bagel Store was well-appointed with olive green walls, stainless steel chairs and customer tables carved from natural wood. Live plants were placed on every table and watered once a week. Atop the wall above the counters were three-dimensional letters made of sheet metal in an assortment of colors and font styles. Together, it spelled out the name of the store like a marquee. It suited the eclectic nature of the Pacific Northwest. Two menu boards were backlit. The wall on one side of the store was covered with posters of upcoming concerts, plays, marathons and social events in Seattle and the surrounding areas. The posters were replaced once a month by a marketing company which was paid by event organizers to distribute their print materials and publicize their events. I felt like all of these contributed to the ambiance of the store that I likened to a concession stand of an independent movie theater.

A strong and organic sense of community was built by the customers themselves. The Bagel Store became the nearby residents' gathering place to meet up and spend time with family, friends and co-workers.

The space was 1,600 square feet and located on a corner lot. The floor-to-ceiling windows faced the east so sunlight cascaded and enveloped the space in the mornings, perfect for a breakfast diner. The inside layout was arranged to optimize customer flow, streamline the ordering process and maximize the real estate. In the center was the bagel case or display cabinet with baskets carrying each kind of bagel. When we opened in the morning, the baskets would be filled to the brim with mounds of freshly baked bagels for the day.

Besides this, we had beverage fridges, a cold case that displayed special items and a grab-n-go fridge for cream cheese spreads that we mixed in-house. We had shelves for bags of chips and sleeves of bagels.

We utilized the service counters with an espresso machine, drip coffee machine, coffee grinders, blenders, toasters, microwave ovens and a countertop convection oven, along with various supplies, packaging materials, and paper and plastic products.

On the right side of the bagel case was the sandwich fridge where we had all of the ingredients needed by the employees to prepare the made-to-order sandwiches. On the left side was the register and beverage station. In the corner of the room was a self-service station with a television mounted on the wall. It was turned on the news channel or the kids' channel, along with music that played from the sound system all through the day.

In the back was the kitchen where every bit of space was utilized as well. There was a walk-in cooler that we kept well-stocked and organized. There was an attached proofer and oven along with baking and transport racks. The machinery we used most included a professional-grade slicer and a giant mixer. We also had a triple sink, a hand sink and a dishwasher to the benefit and relief of the employees.

CHAPTER 6

2016

2016 WAS A DIFFICULT YEAR on a personal level. I had a new business just over a year old that needed attending to and cultivating. I worked seven days a week for the first two years of business, but I was used to it. It became second nature. Wake then bake. My only days off were our four non-working holidays in the calendar year: Thanksgiving Day, Christmas Day, New Year's Day, and Easter Sunday. Even then, I was probably working from home or setting up seasonal decorations in the store.

On the home front, my dad was diagnosed with a serious health condition. The doctors found a brain tumor. My attention was divided between my responsibility to my business and my family. It was difficult because logically, I had to prioritize my business, which was a big investment and the source of income that I relied on. I also had employees that depended on their jobs as their source of income. But in the back of my mind, I had to contend with what was going on with my family that was far away. I couldn't do much about that. It was a difficult position to be in, particularly for a new business owner who had yet to recover his initial investment.

In one instance, my judgment was so impaired with everything that was going on that I messed up. That day, the blueberry bagels were missing from the bagel delivery. Ordinarily, it wouldn't have been a big deal, and I would probably have just not baked blueberry bagels for the next few days. However, I called up the supplier and asked if I could pick up the missing blueberry bagels from the warehouse. I drove to the warehouse and picked up five wooden boards of blueberry bagels. I was on the I-5 on my way back when I crashed into another car and caused a pileup. I didn't hit my brakes in time because my attention was somewhere else. I never got all the cornmeal out of my car. (Cornmeal was used to prevent the bagels from sticking to the boards).

I would fly home to support my parents, usually for a couple of weeks at a time, when the right conditions aligned. These were times when there was enough manpower to make up for my absence at the store. I did this back and forth for a few months. The employees were relatively new as well. Every time I would come back, it looked like a tornado had struck the store. It was a cycle of things being left behind or undone and getting things back in shape. Thankfully though, sales did not suffer. Business actually picked up while I was gone. There was a direct correlation between sales trends and employees' availability when some of them were off from school and could pick up more shifts at the Bagel Store.

Thankfully, things slowly improved and got resolved on the personal side. However, my dad was not the same again and needed more care as an aging parent.

Processing unfamiliar information or facing situations without a clear course of action can feel like a hazy blur. Compartmentalization was a powerful tool I utilized a lot in those days. When I was at work, I would just focus on what was in front of me and not get distracted by the other things going on in my life. Out of sight, out of mind.

THE APARTMENT

When I started the bagel business, I needed to move somewhere near the store so that I could be there at a moment's notice. For the first two years of business, I rented a place to live in. Then I stumbled upon an apartment for sale that fit my criteria. Fortune struck, and I purchased my first property. Owning my place of residence was one of the goals I accomplished through the business. Later on, the broker who helped me became an acquaintance, and their son even came to work at the Bagel Store.

I was able to purchase a small two-bedroom apartment within walking distance of the Bagel Store. It was on the first floor of a three-story apartment building. It was important that the apartment was accessible for my parents when they came to visit and stay with me. The location of this apartment was not scenic by any means but it was practical and got the job done.

The apartment was carpeted. I don't like carpeting because it is hard to clean and maintain. The only professional renovation I did before moving in was replacing the carpet with composite wood flooring. Before I moved in, I met a neighbor who lived on the third floor. He introduced himself and said that he was on the HOA's board. I gathered from that brief interaction that he wanted to tell me something but didn't. A week or so later, I got a letter from the HOA. It contained a notice that stated I had violated the HOA agreement and house rules by removing the carpet. It instructed me to reinstall carpeting in my apartment immediately, after the wood flooring had already been completed.

The notice came with pictures of the renovation shot from the windows of my apartment. It also contained the page in the HOA agreement that pertained to the flooring restriction. The page stated that removing the carpet from an apartment required HOA approval. I felt some way about it, truth be told. I remember thinking what a nice and welcoming neighbor I had!

I went through the resale certificate documents I was given when I purchased the apartment in order to look for anything that could help me. I found out that the documents the board gave me were slightly different. Most likely it was a new version of the HOA agreement. The version I was given stated that the flooring could be changed with permission of the owner of the unit who lived directly under the apartment. Well, I was on the first floor with no unit under it, so no permission was needed. There was no one to be bothered by any footsteps or noises.

I responded to the letter from the HOA and included the HOA agreement I was given. Some weeks later, the HOA responded and conceded that the wood flooring was permissible. They also mailed me a copy of the newer version with the updated section that they had referenced in the original notice.

When faced with a problem like this, I try to keep my composure and find documentation to support my argument. It is hard for others to argue against you if there is irrefutable evidence backing your claim.

HUMAN RESOURCE MANAGEMENT

My approach to hiring and training new employees evolved over time. My success rate was 50%. One of two hires would work out on average. In the first few years, my tactics were very intensive. There was even a span of time at the Gelato Shop when I prepared a rigorous two-week training schedule for new customer service associates. I dedicated my time to that, teaching them the history of the owners and the company, the history of gelato, and the difference between gelato and ice cream. That didn't last too long. Those trainees quit straight away.

I learned that hiring for entry-level positions is a crapshoot. Sometimes you get lucky and hire someone good, and other times not. A job interview or checking references can give you an indication of an applicant's viability, but you can't ever be sure until they are on the floor. A particular example was when I called one applicant's references. Their former manager just confirmed that they worked there and did not offer any other information. I didn't read between the lines and proceeded to hire them. Big mistake. A good interview doesn't necessarily correlate to a good employee. By the same token, I had amazing employees who had awful interviews where they seemed disengaged and disinterested. After a while, I would just hedge my bets and hire two people for a single job vacancy. On the rare occasion that both new hires worked out, then great. I wouldn't have to hire the next time there was a job vacancy.

Over time, I changed how we trained new employees. It became more casual and relaxed. I would first schedule them as an extra person and just invest in them by doing more training over a longer span of time. In this regard; they could absorb information by osmosis like a sponge. They would learn just by being in the environment. The longer they worked in the store, the more we could see their personality and whether they would fit in (or not fit in) with the team. Typically, I would let the regular staff train them on the job to make it more natural and less intense. The new hire would shadow them for the first few days. Afterwards, the regular staff would shadow the new hire to double-check that what they were doing was correct.

After the first forty hours, they were then expected to work independently and do the tasks that were assigned to them. Only then would they get tips, which motivated them to complete their tasks every day and adhere to work and attendance standards. At that point, we were better able to assess whether they were a good fit for the store. Likewise, the new person could assess whether the store was a good fit for them. The relationship between employer and employee is reciprocal, after all. I would do an hour of review training with them after their initial training to review their knowledge, ensure accuracy and precision, and offer suggestions to make their work easier, faster, and more efficient.

The review training covered many reminders for many small things: Wipe the knife between uses, especially if going from savory to sweet or vice versa. Spread the strawberry cream cheese thinner because it is runnier. Slice the bagel right away after applying the spread because the longer you leave it, the softer the cream cheese becomes, making it messier to slice. Make sure to differentiate between "lox and cream cheese" and "lots of cream cheese." If a customer says just plain, confirm if they meant plain cream cheese or nothing on the dry bagel. And so on.

I reminded them of the items with similar sounding names so they wouldn't get confused by them: Veggies with cream cheese or veggie flavored cream cheese, salmon lox with cream cheese or salmon flavored cream cheese, tuna salad sandwich or tuna cheddar melt, pastrami deli sandwich or pastrami Reuben melt, honey ham deli sandwich or just ham.

I had guidelines on how to ring up custom orders: One, if debating between different ways to charge an order, choose the option where you press the least number of buttons on the register. Two, hone in on the main component of the sandwich and start from there. There were lots of little things that could get lost, so information like this needed to be transferred to each staff member. The devil is in the details.

EMPLOYEE LIFECYCLE

Employee retention in the Bagel Store was buoyed by tips, scheduling, and employee stickiness.

Since the organization was mostly flat, the employees watched over and called one another out if anyone was not pulling their weight or adhering to standards. Fairness—or equally important, the perception of fairness—is always a big, ongoing facet in a group of people working together. For the Bagel Store, this resonated because the tips were split evenly among staff based on number of hours worked, not how much or little each employee contributed. This wouldn't be fair if one person did most of the work but was still compensated similarly to their peers. Tips were important to motivate attendance and facilitate employee retention, as the staff received them on the same day that they worked. It encouraged them to be punctual and ready to work on a consistent and reliable basis. This was a great tool for me as an employer.

There were a few employees that were terminated. They were mostly full-time workers who were let go with cause. Others were lacking or not a good fit in our work culture, so we just stopped putting them on the schedule or limited their shifts. They were given less priority on the schedule but acted as back-ups or floaters in case there was no one else available to work. It was always a good idea to keep the relationship friendly and positive.

I controlled and released the work schedule every Friday. The employees gave me their monthly availability; the days and times that they could work that month. I would typically work around their schedule and take into account everybody's availability. Staff with consistent availability got a fixed schedule. Staff with other commitments or priorities had a flexible schedule. Having the schedule that they wanted also contributed significantly to employee retention.

I have a pragmatic view of people. They tend to be better behaved if they know that you are not dependent on them. If they know that you are dependent on them, they think they can get away with more. It was always better for me to keep a larger employee pool or be overstaffed than the opposite. You also need to weigh the cost of overstaffing versus the cost of hiring and training. From my point of view, hiring and training is more costly. It requires a more significant but also more uncertain investment. If you can't afford to pay a higher salary, then you can't afford to hire and train someone new.

Over the years, I identified a profile that seemed to indicate that an applicant or new hire would do well and fit in with the rest of the team. Interpersonal dynamics, even in such a small organization, can be complicated and complex. There were cliques, friendships, groups, and subgroups that formed. For the most part of my tenure, the staff was friendly with one another, and they also developed bonds that extended outside of the workplace, where they engaged in activities together. Stickiness refers to employees striking healthy and positive connections with their peers in a conducive work environment. Those employees stayed longer than their counterparts who did not form bonds with their co-workers.

Most of the time, employees will have problems either with each other or their boss. I would actually prefer they had a problem with me because I don't need to work with them directly for them to do their job correctly. Bonding over disliking the boss is alright with me if it doesn't affect the quality of work.

In my experience, the store had "generations" of team members, as I liked to call it. Each "generation" generally lasted two years after which the makeup of the team would change for the most part.

PRICING

Pricing is a fluid question that every business owner has to contend with on an ongoing basis. Most years, we just implemented an annual price increase across the board and committed to that pricing for as long as possible. I would conduct comparative pricing by finding out the prices of bagels in the higher-end supermarkets, so I knew how our pricing compared to those benchmarks.

My personal philosophy is that pricing is too low when no one complains. People have different levels of price tolerance or sensitivity, so if the least tolerant customers don't even complain, your product is priced too low. Some of the customers would initially complain but they would get used to the new prices after a while.

For me, it is acceptable if 10% of customers complain. This is an indicator that I am making a profit, and at worst, losing 10% of sales doesn't significantly affect the bottom line. It might even be offset by reducing direct food and labor costs.

The Bagel Store could be categorized as a "cash cow." We made decent money but operated in a mature industry. In order to broaden the market, we would have had to grow inorganically, like expanding to different locations or opening new or non-traditional sales channels. I ran a very straightforward operation. We didn't offer deliveries, online orders or third-party orders. We didn't push catering or promotional events outside of the store.

Another important aspect was the impact of price increases from the supplier and vendor side, which also had to be taken into consideration. I mostly accepted the price increases from our suppliers and vendors. For the most part, they seemed fair and justified. I understood that they were running for-profit businesses of their own. They also needed to make a profit in order to stay in business.

Service providers like janitorial suppliers, insurance or utilities (cable, phone, internet, credit card processing services) were always trickier. As a rule, you should always negotiate, as they expect you to counter their price increase, and they factor that into their initial offer. I often needed to negotiate with them because they presented outrageous price increases that seemed unreasonable. For credit card merchant services, the usual way to get more competitive pricing was to re-sign new contracts with them for one to three-year terms. (Three years is a long time to be stuck with a vendor but is not outside of the norm.)

I've come across my fair share of good service providers that had fair prices and bad ones that took advantage of their customers. I had a memorably bad experience with a janitorial supplies company. They were not only priced higher than industry standards, but they also did not provide satisfactory or even adequate service. I neglected to see the fine print in their agreement. It was an evergreen contract that automatically renewed for another three-year term if you didn't give them a notice of cancellation. Outside of that short window, they had a firm grip on you. The fine print is not fine for the customer at all.

A sales representative from a rival provider came to the Bagel Store to get our business. They asked to look at the contract. They verbally assured me that it was expired and that I had no obligation to stay with the other company. This rival company was reputable and they presented us with cheaper and more attractive terms and conditions.

I was made aware after the fact that the old service provider of janitorial supplies was seeking payment for the full term that had just automatically renewed. For all three years. They threatened a legal course of action. In the end, we agreed to settle. I paid two or three months' worth of service fees. It was an important if not expensive lesson to be sure.

Don't sign a contract or make important decisions right away, especially when your judgment might be impaired, like at night or when you're emotional, tired, or under duress. Sleep on it. Take the time to weigh the consequences and analyze all the dimensions of what you are signing or doing.

CHAPTER 7

2017

THE GOAL HAD ALWAYS BEEN to grow the business and open more stores. Two years passed of running the Bagel Store. Things were going smoothly, so I thought it was the perfect opportunity and the right time to grow my legal entity, Mober LLC, by purchasing a second store. I would do what I did the first time and follow the same process.

The first option that would have been simpler or more logical would have been to expand and replicate the Bagel Store into a second location. Perhaps that would have yielded even better results in the end. However, in my head, the greatest advantage of the Bagel Store was possibly also its biggest risk: the bagel supplier. We received the product twice or thrice a week as bagel pucks (raw, pre-shaped dough). This made labor easier and less complicated than a traditional bakery. All we had to do was add the finishing touches, proof, and steam bake the bagels in the morning.

While our supplier was dependable and the quality of both the product and service was consistent, I saw it as a potential risk to be completely reliant on a single supplier. Should the company go sideways or the relationship sour, I would have more or even everything to lose. My thought process was to diversify the risk and try another business concept.

The first opportunity that presented itself was a wholesaler of natural fruit sweeteners. They sold their product through their website, other ecommerce platforms, and some retail locations like Whole Foods. Their office and warehouse were located only minutes away from my existing place of business. How perfect was this? The asking price was reasonable, although they were just breaking even year over year. It seemed to me that the problem was volume. They were not making enough sales to offset their expenses and make a profit. It could also have been high manufacturing costs from the co-packer or delivery costs from the freight. I had wholesale experience from the Gelato Shop, so I believed that I was equipped to operate the business successfully. I thought it would be the right fit and a perfect second business concept to complement the Bagel Store.

I approached the business purchase the same way I did my first successful deal. I was methodical and cordial to the seller to show him that I was experienced and knew what I was doing. Looking back, it seemed like this particular seller was hesitant and tentative in our interactions.

In the end, the purchase did not close because the seller decided to go with another buyer. Afterwards, I reflected on why this opportunity did not pan out.

I think the purchase price for the Bagel Store was high, so that allowed me the luxury of being methodical, slow, and careful. This business, on the other hand, had a more competitive asking price that didn't provide a barrier against other offers. This played more into the seller's favor because it gave them the ability to choose the easier and less conscientious buyer—if their motivation was to close the sale as fast as possible. Perhaps they were hiding something they did not want the potential buyer to discover, so they just priced it on the lower end. Or perhaps they simply received a higher bid from another buyer. Regardless, I was dejected that the deal did not close. If I had the experience that I did later, I wouldn't have given up so easily. I would put a more competitive offer on the table. I would have done more to move the needle and convince the seller that I was the right buyer. Even if it didn't change his mind, nothing worse could have happened.

The next business opportunity was a grill located in a nearby business park. I met with the owner. He seemed to like me. We had a verbal agreement that he would sell this store to me. I was feeling confident about this, but after a few days, I got an email from the seller's broker stating that the seller had decided to go forward with a different buyer. It might have been for the best. This business always switched hands after several months. I'm not sure if it was the location that was wrong. I suspected the business brokers were not ethical. Perhaps they intentionally chose the wrong buyers so they can repeat being the brokers and earn multiple commissions on the same listing.

And so, when the next opportunity came along, I swung to the other side of the pendulum and acted more aggressively. My top-of-mind strategy was to be an easy buyer and accommodate the seller as much as I could. I went with the intent to close the deal as quickly and smoothly as possible. I would just sort out the new store's problems after the purchase had been closed. My previous experiences taught me that anything can happen before a deal is closed, and I didn't want to lose another opportunity after having lost a handful due to being too careful.

My experience during this time made me realize that people don't necessarily learn from experience. It's not as elementary as that. Instead, previous experiences and their outcomes shape and color the decisions that we make in the future. I was conservative with the Bagel Store purchase and the deal closed, so I persisted on the same track. I was conservative with the sweetener wholesaler and the grill. Those deals did not close, so I course corrected and became more aggressive in the next instance. I was aggressive with purchasing my second business, and the deal closed because of that. (Later on though, the experience I had with my second business was not the most positive. And so, with the next one, my mindset will be to err on the side of caution again.)

I finally bought my second store, a French Bakery, in 2017, using a loan I had successfully secured for this business expansion. Although the Bagel Store and the French Bakery might have seemed similar from afar, they could not have been more different. For one, the French Bakery was more reliant on labor and less so on the supplier. My intention to diversify risk and limit the critical component worked in that regard. I had a meeting with the pastry chef before the deal closed, and I found her to be knowledgeable and a great asset to the French Bakery.

THE FRENCH BAKERY

The French Bakery was located in a bustling town square in a city outside of Seattle. It was inside a building that had a modern architecture and incorporated flora and natural elements in its design. It was thirty minutes to an hour away from where I lived depending on the time of day. Luckily, my commute was counter flow to the traffic most of the time. At 1,200 square feet, it was a smaller space than the Bagel Store though the rent per square footage was higher. Outside were a couple of metal tables and chairs that were reminiscent of a French Bistro.

Inside, original artwork and replications of paintings dotted the canary yellow walls. It had lacquered, heavy tables and chairs with the outline of a cup of coffee cut out from the backrest. One side of the space was dedicated to the service area where an assortment of refrigerated and room temperature pastries lined the counters and display cases. Behind, the menu was written on a giant chalkboard that covered the back wall. We had an A-frame chalkboard for specials. We had shelves that were filled top to bottom with syrup bottles, tea jars and ceramic ware.

In the back was the kitchen which was utilized pretty well

by the bakers. The night baker started their shift before midnight and the day baker ended their shift by 6 PM. That meant there was at least one baker in the kitchen eighteen hours a day, seven days a week.

While there were some customers who stayed inside the cafe to take a respite from the busy world or a break away from their busy lives, most of the customers just grabbed a box of pastries to take home or to the office.

More so than the Bagel Store and the Gelato Shop, the space was only secondary to the products we made and sold. The French Bakery was both a traditional boulangerie that makes traditional French breads and a patisserie that makes pastries, cakes and tarts. Some of the items you can see on a given day include an assortment of: brioche, puff pastries, pithiviers, strudel, scones, muffins and cookies. For breads, there were baguette, wild rice and onion, whole wheat and honey, cinnamon swirl, braided challah, focaccia, Kalamata olive and rosemary, roasted garlic, and dinner rolls. For sweets, there were macarons, eclairs, bread pudding, crème brulee, tiramisu, Paris-brest, Marie Antoinette, Religieuse, Fraisier cake, Opera cake, Tarte Tropezienne, Dacquoise torte, Sacher, Balcarce and Concord cake. There was cheesecake though some customers complained that they are not French.

Holidays were special. Seasonal items were available to the delight and frenzy of the customers. For Christmas, there were Kugelhopf, Stollen, Buche de Noel, gingerbread houses and gingerbread men. For Valentine's, there were chocolate strawberries, pink Madelines and various heart decorated or strawberry flavored desserts. Mothers' Day and Easter were critical days for signature and specialty cake orders.

THE PASTRY CHEF

Like a nightmare unfolding slowly, some things came out after the deal was closed. The pastry chef, who was also the head baker and manager of the store, already had plans to leave the store. The absentee owners knew this. The baker also claimed that she owned some of the fixtures and furniture on the asset list that had been included in the sale. She took her equipment from the store, and I now had to replace it all. I questioned whether the asset list that had been presented to me was accurate.

There were red flags in hindsight. She was nowhere to be found on the day of closing. She was incommunicado when we called her phone. But when you have rose-colored glasses on, red flags are just flags.

I was not as fortunate with the labor situation at the French Bakery as I had been with the supplier situation at the Bagel Store. Shortly after purchasing the French Bakery, I had a meeting with the pastry chef. This was when she told me that she would be leaving in a matter of months. Moreover, she would be taking all of the other bakers that worked in the store with her. She was planning to open her own bakery. My heart just dropped. I suspect that part of her seed money came from the proceeds of the sale of the store that the absentee owners gave her.

What I had not known were a couple of things: French pastry chefs are notoriously egotistic. I would say with confidence that most of them desire to procure their own bakery, where they can do what they want to. They are also very hierarchical in nature. They place a great deal of value on their training, which extends as loyalty to the person who they trained with. They will follow this person wherever they go.

My natural first instinct is diplomacy and to resolve things as amicably as I can. I tend to acquiesce to other people's needs and wants. After all, this method worked so well in my first business. I am water and have a go-with-the-flow approach. Don't rock the boat and just see what happens. People are assets to a company, but they are never part of the purchase when you buy a business, so be prepared for any outcome in that regard. And so, I didn't put up a fight and made it very easy for the baker to do as she pleased.

Now I know that different places or situations call for different approaches. Looking back, I believe I would have benefited more from being like a rock and taking a firm approach. Honestly, the outcome might have been more favorable had the staff been fired outright and replaced. Instead, it was as if a knife was dangling over my head for the duration of my ownership of the French bakery. There was a constant threat looming on the horizon. The staff had power over me, since they could walk away at any given time.

Just like she said she would, the pastry chef left within a few months to take a short trip to France for a break and to gather inspiration. She would prepare to open her own shop afterwards. In the meantime, she left her staff in my business like it was a daycare until they were ready to pack up and start working at her new bakery. They needed somewhere to work and earn livable income for the moment, after all. Funnily enough, I would always see the pastry chef in my kitchen at the store, idly hanging around with the other bakers. I found it hypocritical because she told me once that bakers are always busy in the kitchen and that they shouldn't be distracted because baking requires a lot of focus and attention.

The pastry chef also recommended her replacement, which I naively agreed to. I thought she would still have the French Bakery's best interest at heart, considering she had worked there for many, many years. The replacement she picked was bad (and crazy) of course. His background was as a chocolatier, but he did not have the finesse to produce quality work. We asked him to bring desserts to his interview, and they were good, but they were probably desserts he was capable of making in a contained environment—or perhaps he didn't even make them. He later resigned, claiming he made more money from unemployment.

Once again, I was reliant on the old pastry chef and her people. I decided to promote her right-hand person to the position of head baker and gave her a substantial raise, hoping that might convince her to stay. She appreciated it but remained non-committal. I hired new bakers who could make cakes, as the pastry chef hadn't trained any of her subordinates to make cakes. That was her trump card so that she would always be irreplaceable and invaluable to the store. It was also a way to influence and control her team, as there were still things left for her to teach them.

Later on, I found a pastry chef that I liked (whom the old pastry chef did not approve of, naturally). He had the experience, background, and ability to do the job. However, there was no buy-in from the old chef's bakers. The team dynamics between them were impossible, as the staff knew that he was a threat to them and their old boss. He was efficient with his time and production work, and he was used to working in small teams.

My problems didn't end there. This new pastry chef I wanted to hire also had designs of his own. He said that he wanted a partnership and to be co-owner of the store as a condition of accepting the job. The original pastry chef didn't say it outright, but I think her intent had also been to squeeze me so that I would offer her a stake in the French Bakery. It was impossible to work with her, so I never broached the subject. My takeaway is that the world of French bakeries is cutthroat, and everyone wants something out of you.

I politely declined the new pastry chef's offer. Maybe in the future when we have worked together, I could have agreed to it. However, I can't have someone I barely know as a business partner. He went on his way to co-own a small pizzeria. Meanwhile, his wife started to work with me part time to make cakes and macarons. The window between the store and him was still open.

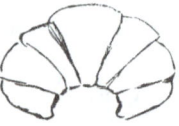

CHAPTER 8

2018

2018 WAS THE MOST PHYSICALLY and mentally demanding year in business for me. I had to juggle the Bagel Store and the French Bakery. Although they seemed similar in nature, they were complete opposites. The Bagel Store was the model child who ate their vegetables and said their please and thank-yous. The French Bakery was the problem child who chugged energy drinks and stayed up all night playing video games.

I tried to integrate the two stores in a few ways, like selling some of the French Bakery's products in the Bagel Store. Effectively, the French Bakery had the Bagel Store as its wholesale customer. I scheduled some of the Bagel Store's employees to work at the French Bakery so there were more shifts and job diversity for them as well.

I changed my schedule at the Bagel Store, which I had owned

for around four years at that point. I used to work there full time, but I reduced my responsibilities to accommodate the French Bakery. Luckily, I had staff who had been working at the Bagel Store for some time. They could keep an eye out for me. They knew how I operated the store and could pick up the slack of my workload. In my new schedule that year, I would still go to the Bagel Store around 5 a.m. in the morning and leave for the French Bakery when it opened at 7 a.m. Like some bakeries you may have observed, the baker would leave after baking for the day, and the staff would take care of the customers. The rest of my responsibilities at the Bagel Store I could take care of remotely. One cold winter day, I finished my bake at the Bagel Store. I hurriedly headed out the door to drive to the French Bakery when I slipped on some black ice. I stayed like that on my back in the dark parking lot for a minute. I looked up at the pitch black sky and thought, "I have to get going".

With the pastry chef leaving, the French Bakery was under-staffed. I took over some of the kitchen work like baking pastries and preparing made-to-order sandwiches. I also served customers, closed up the shop, and made coffee in the front of house. The hardest part about learning to barista is frothing the milk. I can tell whether the milk is being steamed correctly by the sound that it makes. A high-pitched sound is not good. A low-pitched, whirring sound is music to my ears. You can control how dry or wet the milk will be by where you place the tip of the steam wand. If it's closer to the surface, the milk will be frothier or dry. You can achieve this by gently lowering the frothing pitcher (making sure the steam wand never leaves the milk) while tilted away from your face. A perfect cappuccino is so nice.

Aside from these tasks, my major responsibilities were shopping, hiring, schedule, payroll, and bookkeeping. I cross-posted the Bagel Store employees to the French Bakery, but none of them liked it because it was a different work style and environment. Most of all, it was because the tips were structured differently. At the Bagel Store, the employees got their tips on the same day that they worked. At the French Bakery, they got their tips on payday along with their wages. This was because the night bakers participated in the tip pool, so it had to be distributed evenly.

My role was filling in the gaps that needed filling. Most of the kitchen duties I took on were easy enough and did not require a lot of training or practice. These included simple tasks like mixing pastry cream filling, cutting and shaping dough, and putting together different kinds of tarts and bread pudding. By taking these relatively easy but time-consuming tasks off the staff's hands, they had more time to focus on making the more technical items. The pastry chef taught me a universal lesson that is true of any bakery kitchen: A place for everything, and everything in its place. All supplies and materials have to go where they belong. Bakeries are hard work. Being orderly and organized goes a long way when there are a lot of bakers in the kitchen.

I learned to fill the pastry cases and always make them look full and presentable. I would cashier, barista, and close the store. I even acted as the handyman or called in for repairs when I was in over my head. It was an old store, so the equipment seemed to rotate between needing parts, replacements, or repairs. After closing time, I would spend hours in the bakery at night to prep for the next day so that there would be things to sell in the morning. Then I would get Chinese take-out from next door before driving back home.

We were generating revenue and selling out of products, but our turnover remained lower than the sales history the previous owner had given me. Our production couldn't meet the demand, which I suppose is a better problem to have. It wasn't an easy fix though. Even so, I hit a milestone and had my highest sales of the year with the two stores combined at $1,000,000. The two stores' bookkeeping was kept separate, with each store categorized as its own location and P&L. This I also learned from my experience at the Gelato Shop.

I think it all boiled down to pricing, specifically in how it related to labor cost. The French Bakery's pricing was just too low compared to the labor and materials it took to make the product. It was hard to determine the acceptable and appropriate price for each item because there were so many varieties. The preparation for each was different, not to mention the food and labor cost involved. You would have had to conduct a time-and-motion study in order to determine the right, sustainable prices.

For example, a raspberry tart was priced at $6. However, a pack of raspberries already cost $6, and each pack only had enough for two or three raspberry tarts. This was because the bakers were taught to pack them in tightly in order to make them look appealing. Added to that, we made the pastry crust and pastry cream from scratch, so margins were slim. Of course, the bakers were not concerned with the commerce part of the bakery. Their job and motivation were just to make the product as nice as possible.

That was the main reason why the French Bakery eked out a small profit. Something was wrong with the pricing, even before considering the variance of wastage, human mistakes, unsold products, and the deviation of actual from standard. The fundamentals had to be changed for it to work. I didn't think I was the person who could make those changes.

THE LEASE RENEWAL

The five-year lease for the Bagel Store expired that year. I still had two five-year lease options left, which would last until 2028. I thought it would be a relatively simple process, as the lease stated how the new rent amount would be calculated. Of course, I underestimated my landlord. They required my guarantors on the first lease, the previous owners of the Bagel Store, to re-sign the lease renewal agreement. There was no incentive for them or anyone to do that. I appealed to their sense of decency anyway as previous owners, especially as I still had a good relationship with my supplier. I offered to sign something to the effect that they could have the Bagel Store if something happened to me and I defaulted on the lease. In that way, they wouldn't be taking on any risk whatsoever.

One weekend after working a tiring double shift at the Bagel Store and the French Bakery, the supplier called me to the factory. He sounded encouraging on the phone. I drove all the way there, optimistic for some good news. He had a counter offer. They would sign the lease renewal. In exchange, they would substantially increase the cost of the bagels equivalent to the savings I would get from the rent with them as guarantors.

I was livid. It felt to me like they were taking advantage of the vulnerable position that I was in. It also contributed to the feeling that everyone wanted to get something from me. It triggered the same feeling when dealing with the pastry chef. That was the only time I shared a negative opinion with my supplier. I was cranky and tired, so I gave him a piece of my mind. I went back to the landlord expressing that the guarantors would not re-sign the lease renewal. I figured that they knew that. They knew I wasn't a risk factor, as I was a reliable tenant with a proven history. They just wanted to raise the rent. I was able to sign the new lease with an acceptable rent without any guarantors this time. Luckily, my relationship with the supplier was still good. I believe he also realized that the way he had gone about it was not very cool.

GENERAL & ADMINISTRATIVE DUTIES

A business operator needs to follow a routine that is sensible and works for them. I set up a small office and filing system from home. From there, I kept my data & password sheets, performed my administrative tasks and checked off on my list of things to do.

On Mondays, I placed orders to the juice, milk, salmon and bagel vendors for deliveries for the week. On Fridays, I placed a second bagel order for the Monday delivery. On Sundays, I counted inventory at the Bagel Store for the next week's orders. The head baker prepared the inventory count and placed the vendor orders for the French Bakery. I did shopping trips to Restaurant Depot and Business Costco twice or thrice a week for both stores.

On the first day of the month, I did the payroll for the pay period, mailed rent checks and paid bills. On the fifteenth day of the month, I did the payroll for the pay period and paid more bills. On the twenty-fifth day of the month, I filed the sales tax returns, scheduled credit card payments and reconciled accounts on Quickbooks. At the end of the year, I cleaned out my filing cabinet and transferred all of the records in storage boxes.

REPAIR AND MAINTENANCE

The natural, constant state of a small business is that of entropy—breakdowns and repairs. This is the norm for a store. It is a lucky day if things go as planned or expected. There is always something that needs to be fixed, repaired, replaced, or upgraded.

We had our routine maintenance, which mainly involved wiping down dust on the coils or filters of the cold equipment. There were also electrical, plumbing, HVAC, appliance, and tech repairs. It is critical to document such problems whenever they occur, including the steps taken to address them and which ones worked and which ones didn't. They are never one-time occurrences. If it happened once, it is likely you will encounter the same problem again at some point in time. I feel like anything that could have happened to that business happened to me. An expensive repair was replacing the heat exchanger in our attached oven. It was an old model, so I had to hunt down the part that was compatible with it. You just have to find a way, either as a workaround, a Band-Aid, or a long-term, permanent solution. As the owner, the buck stops with you.

Once, the Bagel Store was broken into. The security system caught the burglar on camera around 10 p.m. They were only inside the store for several seconds. They smashed the glass door and tried to grab the cash register. After realizing that it was bolted down, the perpetrator fled. I came in at 5 a.m. the next day to bake. When I drove into the lot, I just thought it was strange that the lights were on. Then I saw people inside the shop. I didn't even notice the front door's glass everywhere. I think that early in the morning, you just don't register such an unusual picture. You're not awake enough to get too frightened or nervous to drive away. I walked in casually, and the men inside introduced themselves as detectives. The police had driven by at night and saw what happened. Three stores in the commercial center had been broken into. They briefed me on what happened, asked me some questions, and requested surveillance footage.

It turned out to be a burglary ring. Their target was the cash registers, and they managed to steal the ones from the other stores that had been hit. A few months later, I got notified that suspects from the case were being held in custody. The detectives found them through traffic-light cameras. Their phones had been on that night, so the police were able to track their movements at the time of the burglary, confirming that they were in the vicinity. When they were apprehended, hard evidence was also found against them.

Another time, a person walked into the French Bakery. There was only one employee working at the time. This was near closing, and this store only had one closer at night. They asked the employee to get a first-aid kit, and the employee went to the back to retrieve it. While the person was alone in the front and no one was looking, he reached into the tip jar, took out all the money, and dashed. The poor employee was crying when she called me. I felt for her for being victimized. Although she was safe, it does mess with your head when something like that happens to you. It's the feeling of being taken advantage of and not being able to do anything about it.

Another time, a person locked themselves in the restroom and wouldn't come out. I looked at my phone and saw a flurry of messages, missed calls, and voicemails. The staff was trying to reach me. They couldn't close because there was someone in the restroom. They saw him doing something unseemly. The person left before the sheriff's office got to the store.

I've learned from my earliest experiences to be cautious of fraud and scams. Any means of contact is a way in for scammers to get to you: phone, mail, email, in person. The real world can be dangerous and insidious. My favorite scam is receiving mail from a private company dressed up as a government agency requiring the business to buy a poster as part of "regulatory compliance." The post office police (a very real and very serious agency) needs to get on that case and persecute the perpetrators for mail fraud.

On the other hand, there are good people out there too. We had multiple instances where staff would forget to lock up for the night. You could simply push the front door and it would open without anyone in the store. Thankfully, nothing ever got stolen. Customers who walked into the store were kind enough to inform our next-door neighbors or call local law enforcement to report that the location was not secure. There are honest people out there who will help a stranger without expecting anything in return.

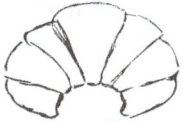

CHAPTER 9
2019

AFTER TWO YEARS OF OPERATION, I figured that enough time had passed, and my only logical course of action was to sell the French Bakery. My other options were to get into a partnership with either of the pastry chefs. In either case, I would lose my equity. I also knew it would be very difficult working with either of the chefs on a daily basis. They were not people I wanted to be business partners with.

It was of utmost importance that no one knew what was going on. Besides it being the standard procedure, I didn't want the other players to make their moves before I could make mine. It was a race of who could pull the trigger first. The old pastry chef was a jackhammer, who would beat you down and wear you out repeatedly with multiple strikes and psychological warfare. At work, I am more like a snake. I can smile to your face but do my work behind the scenes. I wait for my opportunity to strike, but I will make that one shot count. You won't know until it's over. I admit that I have been called insincere. The owner of the Gelato Shop called me that when I left my job. I was offended, but ultimately, I agreed with her assessment years later. It was my survival mechanism and tactic.

I met with the business broker, and he put up the business listing. I was able to secure a buyer and close the deal. That in itself was a success and a victory for me. I was able to execute the exit strategy flawlessly and reach a liquidity event. Thankfully, I maintained a positive relationship with the owners before me. They agreed to re-sign the lease reassignment along with myself. I was relieved by how cooperative they were. They took the position of second guarantors while I, the first.

No matter what anyone says, the process of exiting a business is just as important as the entry or acquisition process. It is part of every business lifecycle, after all. On balance, I recovered my investment and then some. I count it as a notch on my belt, even if the business was in my hands for only a couple of years. My dream had always been to own a cake shop. It didn't turn out how I had hoped it would, but I scratched that itch, kicked it off my bucket list, and got out with minimal damage.

One egregious moment that I will never forget is an email conversation I found between the pastry chef and a job applicant. The applicant disclosed in the email that she had piercings and tattoos and hoped that it would not present a problem. The pastry chef answered, claiming that the owner (namely myself) was a conventional, traditional person and would not hire her. Understand that I worked in food service for years and years. Everyone has tattoos and piercings, and I never had a problem with that. If I did, I wouldn't have had any food-service employees. The applicant expressed disgust in the email and threatened to report the business for discrimination. The pastry chef responded that she was opening her own bakery and that she would like to keep in touch with the applicant and hire her when her bakery opened. This is the type of person I was dealing with. I effectively ended all communication with the pastry chef after my business was settled.

The new owner of the French Bakery replaced all the bakers. I admired his fearless approach, and it turned out he was the better fit for that business. I helped him as much as I could but he became self-sufficient in a very short timeframe. From where I was standing, he was a perfect fit for entrepreneurship.

Now that I had some time on my hands after the French Bakery, I applied that energy to my personal finances and adopted what I had learned from running businesses.

I treated and organized my personal finances as a business. I set up a monthly recurring calendar to reconcile my bank accounts while detecting any fraud activity and paying my monthly bills, credit cards, and mortgage. I combined the numbers in my personal P&L with non-business, passive income like interest from a CD ladder and HYSAs. I compared actual expenses to my personal budget to make sure that I was under or near it. I kept my investment portfolio separate with its own financial statement, as they were long term. I tracked gains or losses, both realized and unrealized, on a monthly basis. I stuck to a broad, long-term investing strategy and didn't deviate from it, only making small adjustments or reallocations from time to time.

EMPLOYEES

I became more conscious of how you can't control people any more than you can control employees. All you can control are your own actions and decisions. I still struggle sometimes, but this thought process freed me from a lot of my own obsessive-compulsive tendencies.

In the fall of 2019, the Bagel Store experienced its highest employee turnover ever. Most of our employees naturally tendered their resignations in the fall; that was just our employee lifecycle. People would go back to school, go out of state, or wait until the end of summer to do something different. That fall, I only had three employees who would stay on, whereas twelve others had given notice. Their last days were spread out across a matter of weeks. I was very, very worried during this time. Most of the staff had just graduated from high school and were moving out of town for college. Others were starting new jobs.

To the outgoing employees' credit, they gave sufficient notice, which I interpreted as their way of making sure the store would be alright. They talked amongst themselves and didn't want to leave the Bagel Store in a bad place. I appreciated their sentiment. I went to work. I was able to hire some good people and rebuild the team over the rest of summer and fall without being understaffed. Some became bridges who only worked for a season until we got more permanent ones who ended up working in the Bagel Store for years. In the end, everything worked out. I rebuilt the staff back to fifteen just in time for winter break, our busiest season of the year. I delegated other work I did like shopping and doing the store's laundry.

CUSTOMERS

We didn't do any advertising for the store like marketing campaigns, promotions, or discounts to attract new customers. Most of our business was from repeat customers, word of mouth, or people who just randomly happened to find the store. However, we participated in local events like charities, fundraisers, and silent auctions when we got asked. Those generated a little publicity and goodwill in the local community. I also donated bagels to the nearby foodbank on a weekly basis and met some lovely people.

I loved our customers at the Bagel Store. They were kind, patient, understanding, and uncomplicated. All they wanted was to hand us their money, get their food, and go. I don't have a problem with that. A significant number of them probably held service jobs at some point, so they were sympathetic to food-service employees. In contrast, the customers at the French Bakery were hard to please. They made a point of giving their opinion on the authenticity of the product or how it was different from the traditional way. "Oh, this isn't how it tasted in Paris." It was funny because the French bakery's profit margins were slimmer. In that way, they were less valuable than my Bagel Store customers. I'm sorry, but that's the truth.

New customers are hard because you don't know if the expectations in their head will match what you are offering them. I prefer that new customers come to me on their own volition rather than me attracting them through a service like Groupon. It feels like if you draw them in, you owe them a favor. Their giving you a chance to earn their business isn't a bad thing, but it is harder to accomplish.

In my opinion, not all customers are worthwhile. I would prefer fewer customers that are easy to please over more customers who are hard to please and cause problems. Make no mistake, I listen to complaints and take feedback seriously in order to improve, as long as the criticism is valid. I also don't offer delivery or online ordering through a third-party vendor. It depends on the owner's priority. Market share and volume was not mine. Resources like inventory or labor dollars are limited. I would rather use them to maximum advantage. It just cuts profits for me and creates more work for less gain.

I'm the kind of owner who listens to the side of the employee and assesses whether they are in the right or not. The customer is not always correct. Due to the nature of my business, I have way fewer employees than customers, and our market is more segmented. This is unlike something like a high-end jewelry shop or a car dealership, where you have one or two large customers that can make or break your business. This is why they place more emphasis on the customers' side and the idea that they are always correct. I suppose it depends on the business you are in.

An employee once asked me what my hobbies were when I wasn't working at the Bagel Store. I thought about it. I told her that when I'm at home, I'm usually doing things like bookkeeping, placing orders, paying bills, doing the payroll or the schedule. I told her that I didn't consider it work because it wasn't stressful for me. She replied that those activities still constituted as work. I don't think I knew my identity outside of the business.

AUDITS AND GOVERNMENT COMPLIANCE

A business owner has to comply with audits that can happen randomly or for cause at any time. They can come from government bodies like the Health Department, Fire Department, Department of Revenue (DOR), Internal Revenue Service (IRS), Employment Security Department (ESD) or Labor & Industry (L&I).

One time, we had a random audit from L&I. They requested proof of hours worked for employees. Thankfully, I knew how to comply with their request. I submitted clock-in and clock-out data retrieved from the POS system; and the payroll register and summary reports from the payroll company for the years that they were auditing. Needless to say, the files were massive. Their intent was to make sure the employee hours worked were accurate and matched what they were paid. After a few months, I received a letter for an in-person meeting in their Everett office. I passed the audit and L&I gave me a check for $80 for payroll tax overpayment. I like to think that it was a small consolation for my inconvenience due to the audit.

Licenses and permits were renewed every year. The Business License, Secretary of State Registration and Food Permit were renewed every April. The Resale Certificate was renewed every four years.

One quirk I found interesting is that Department of Revenue would impose increases in the sales tax rate without communicating it directly to the businesses. This happened twice over many years altogether. There would just be a notice on their website under changes if you cared to look into it. I would prepare the monthly sales tax filing. The sales tax amount I collected from customers and withheld would be lower than the sales tax amount that DOR would collect from the store. Then I would look on the website and see that the sales tax rate had changed. I would only know then to update the sales tax rate on our sales register to reflect the new rate.

Our health inspector's name was Leonard. Throughout my tenure, he gave the Bagel Store a "Good" rating. He always came in to do the unannounced inspection on a Friday at 1 PM after the lunch rush when the store was a mess. God bless Leonard. At least he was consistent and never gave us a rating below Good. One thing to know is the Health Department is required to respond and do a food inspection if a consumer reports the business. This happened once when the particular customer reported the Bagel Store to the Health Department and even posted a scathing review online. Thankfully, the health inspector came and found everything to be in order and compliant with safety standards. I responded to the online review by thanking the customer for their feedback, announcing that we passed the inspection, communicating what happened to the staff and being more mindful with cleaning routines.

CHAPTER 10

2020

WE WERE ALREADY SMASHING our previous years' sales records in January and February of 2020. Business was brisk. By all accounts, it was going to be a record-breaking, banner year. Unbeknownst to everyone, including myself, the world would turn upside down in March. This was an interesting year to be in business, to put it lightly. In hindsight, what I mostly remember about 2020 is that it was the easiest year of operating my business. It didn't feel like it at the time of course.

Before lockdown, we were open seven days a week and nine hours a day. That was how it was for the better part of five years. When the lockdown initially happened, we only stayed open three days a week as an essential business—Friday, Saturday, and Sunday. Customer demand dropped, but these three days were historically our busiest days, and it seemed that supposition would hold during a global epidemic. It made sense to remain open on those days, as we were still breaking even and had enough customers who wanted to get their weekly bagels. In this way, we were also able to move perishable inventory. We still assumed some level of wastage from expired product or spoilage, but they were minimal compared to the alternative had we completely shut down.

We normally had around fifteen employees on the team roster. At the start of the pandemic, I could only retain three employees, while the rest of the staff had to be furloughed. I communicated the situation and everyone understood the reason. The irony was that in the previous fall, the Bagel Store experienced its highest employee turnover ever. I had just hired twelve people in the winter. Then, within only a few months, I had to intentionally pare the staff list down to three again.

Besides the anxiety of the unknown, this was the easiest time for me physically and mentally. Everyone was behaving well, and it was the easiest year to manage people. I think everyone just focused on the present; plans were postponed, and it was hard to make moves for the future. Customers were kind, generous, and understanding. In general, everyone followed the mask policy and social distancing guidelines. It was a difficult time to navigate. People recognized that everyone was just making do with the situation. A few would leave tips that were larger than the amount of money they paid. The world was at a standstill, and so were we.

We had a plan, and we were just riding the crests and waves. Never had there been a year when government had such a direct impact on the workings of the private sector day in and day out. I just didn't want to stick out. My goal was: Don't get on the news. I started each day not knowing how that very same day would end. Employees might test positive for Covid, and we'd just have to make do with what we got. The price of hand sanitizer was wild. It went from $10 to $150 a bottle.

Over the course of the next several months, we added more days of operation, increasing from three to four, then five, then six. As we added new days, I figured I could work by myself the whole day because it would be slow, and most customers wouldn't know that we were open on those days again. It was back to basics. I felt empowered working by myself the whole day like I did when I worked at the Gelato Shop.

Eventually, the employees who were furloughed were brought back. I am very proud to say that everyone who was furloughed came back to work at the Bagel Store when they were invited back. While they were not working, they just claimed unemployment benefits. I received so many unemployment claim letters, even from old employees from years earlier whom I had forgotten about.

One of the things I am most proud of in the history of my business ownership is how all the staff returned and how they trusted me. Sometimes, it can be amazing to work with people if there is good communication and respect on both sides.

None of the Bagel Store's bills, including rent, were forgiven, just deferred. The business bank account never ran dry. And eventually, when cash flow from revenue grew from a trickle to a stream again, all bills were paid. I attributed this to the many years of experience I was able to draw upon: pay bills just on time, control inventory, and connect employee staffing to the sales that we can generate. All of my skills and experience were put to use, including bookkeeping and directing cash flow—money coming in and money going out.

I think it goes to show how an active and present owner can make an enormous impact on their business at a highly consequential level. My ability to be agile, swift, and adaptable, making changes informed by data-driven decisions, enabled the business to stay afloat and navigate the challenges of the rough waters that year. Utilizing hard data, experiential evidence, and instinct all came into play. Keeping a close eye on business needs during tumultuous times is important to optimize cost of goods, labor expenses, and ultimately, the bottom line. It would be very difficult for an absentee owner to do that.

While it was our least profitable year under my ownership, we still managed to yield positive income from operations at the end of the year. What makes a small business interesting is that it is like a recipe that you can refine and fine-tune over time. More revenue doesn't necessarily correspond to more profit. Instead, it is the optimization of revenue over expenses that yields profit.

An unintentional benefit and stroke of luck was that the Bagel Store was positioned more favorably than other businesses (quite literally). We were located in a suburban area, where most of our customers were residents and locals from the city and its surrounding areas. The pandemic had a smaller impact on businesses in the suburbs than on those in commercial and metropolitan areas. Our customers were still there. The stay-at-home and social distancing mandates didn't affect locations like ours as much as they affected the big cities.

To this day, some shops in business and industry areas like business parks and commercial hubs have not fully recovered or have even shut down permanently. Unintended advantages like these make me realize how fortunate I was to be in that position.

Sadly, one of my vendors did not come out on the other side. I have to give credit to all of my vendors and suppliers where it is due. I've had mostly the same vendors over the years of running my business ventures, and they were the best collaborators I can ask for.

From time to time, competitor suppliers and rival service providers would come to the store to curry favor and get our business. They would offer lower price points or different perks, but I didn't seriously entertain them. For me, the long-term relationships I had with existing suppliers were more important. It was more valuable to me to sleep easy at night, knowing and trusting the people and companies I dealt with. I knew I could depend and rely on them when I needed them. Reward your vendors with loyalty, and they will repay you in kind, ideally anyway.

What did I do with the rest of all this free time? I can't stress enough how grateful I am to have been where I was. I enjoyed the fresh air outside on the Snohomish River Trail every chance I got. I worked out from home. I caught up on television shows and listened to music. I called home and reconnected with friends from way back and far away. I was reminded of my favorite lyric by Florence and the Machine, "Regrets collect like old friends", which you start to connect with as you get older.

At the time, I was envious of the small business owners who had gotten out before Covid-19 happened. Now, I'm glad it happened to me and that I'm able to tell the tale. In hindsight, it was an incredible, remarkable, and unforgettable time to be in business, for good and for ill.

INVESTING

While I was dealing with the rocky business landscape, this time was also formative for me as an investor. I continued learning about investing and became my own financial planner. I'm not a certified financial adviser by any means, so these are just my opinions. Take everything I say with a grain of salt.

The most rudimentary way for me to describe the stock market is to use a casino as an analogy. The saying goes, "The house always wins." I think that sentiment applies to the stock market as well. When you are trading stocks and timing the market, your underlying belief is that you are competing against the house, and you think that you can beat it. You think you can outsmart the market. You gain and someone else loses. There is a possibility that may hold true, but more likely than not, you will take hits and losses as well.

One has to understand that the economy and the stock market are two different things. The economy paints a picture of the present using the latest available economic indicators like

GDP and unemployment. The stock market paints a picture of the future based on investor confidence gleaned from the latest earnings calls and companies' performance against expectations. There is a degree of irrationality to it, and so, you cannot apply pure reason or facts. The stock market doesn't exist in a vacuum. The stock market abhors uncertainty. Clarity in the future often leads to optimism.

I personally ascribe to the Jack Bogle philosophy: long-term investments in broad market index funds with a low expense ratio. An index fund is like a basket of stocks or bonds. For example, a Fortune 500 index fund includes all of the companies in the Fortune 500. A NASDAQ index fund includes all of the companies trading in the New York Stock Exchange. A Dow Jones index fund includes the companies in the Dow Jones and so on. Index funds can be specific to an industry, class, or capitalization.

The underlying belief is that you are playing *with* the market. When it wins, you win. When it loses, you lose. Three, ten, or twenty years from now, the market will most likely certainly win even if they say past history doesn't predict future performance. You will make a return on your investment in the long run, even if you only invested at its peaks, as long as you hold and weather the dips, downturns, and recessions. I find that diligent, passive, unemotional investing in a lazy portfolio through dollar-cost averaging work for me.

I learned to detach investing from the news and politics. News cycles last from a day to a week. There will be calamities, natural and manmade. A presidential term is four years. My investing will outlast that, as long as I'm still alive.

CHAPTER 11

2021

IF 2021 HAD A THEME, it was shortage. Specifically, two kinds: supply shortage and labor shortage. I was privy to what was yet to happen to the rest of the world like I had the inside scoop. I experienced firsthand what would soon fill the news cycles: supply chain issues, delays and complications that would impact all facets of commerce.

That's what happens when a giant machine like any organization or the economy comes to a halt. The disruptive event will reverberate across time, its consequences gathering into a tidal wave. Businesses are delicate ecosystems that require equilibrium to survive and thrive.

There was a mismatch between supply and demand in those first two years of the pandemic. In 2020, the supply was there, but the demand was not, as the world stayed home. In 2021, customer demand was reawakening. However, now the supply was not in place due to systemic manufacturing, distribution, and logistical disruptions. The easy balance we were used to before the pandemic was thrown out of order, and there was no quick or easy fix.

Sourcing for the Bagel Store became needlessly complicated, like a treasure hunt. I had no choice but to utilize multiple overlapping vendors and wholesalers in order to build, maintain, and replenish inventory. At the same time, I couldn't overstock because of our limited storage space as well as needing to keep cash flow in check. I would run around different wholesalers in the area like Restaurant Depot and Chef Store (a.k.a. Cash&Carry a.k.a. Smart Foodservice a.k.a. US Foods Store) in a mad dash for something like eggs. At times, they would be out at Restaurant Depot. Other times, they would be out at Chef Store (which got rebranded a few times). Sometimes, Sysco would have them. Sometimes, they would be out of stock. Sometimes, we would substitute liquid eggs with real eggs if they were not available.

Suppliers' deliveries to the Bagel Store also got thrown out of whack, becoming very unpredictable and incremental. Unlike before, there were no guaranteed delivery times, as their drivers and pickers were stretched thin. It was a different driver each week for several months, and so there was no consistency. Staff had to be more careful and double-check when receiving deliveries. It was difficult to prioritize delivery checks because we also had customers who needed to be served at the same time. We had to match received goods with the invoice (which rarely did in those days). There was a lot of going back and forth with our sales reps to make sure we got refunds for items that were charged but not delivered to us.

As a result, a lot of time was spent running between whole-sale distributors. One of our existing suppliers stopped selling the seeds that we used as garnish on our bagels – dehydrated garlic, onion, poppy and sesame. I was able to source it from a different supplier, one I had used earlier at the French Bakery. However, that supplier could not deliver to new customers at that time. They only did "will call" or pick up at their warehouse in downtown Seattle (an hour away).

Like a lot of businesses, our bagel supplier implemented a strategy that year to streamline their operations by having a smaller variety of bagel flavors. This is what's typically done in lean times: scale down inventory and prioritize production runs to the most profitable assets. The owner of the bagel factory reached out to set up a meeting with me. (Not a good sign.) In the meeting, he explained their difficulty delivering product to the store. This was because they took on the legal and financial liability for the driver and the vehicle transporting the bagels. He presented me with two options. One, he offered to sell his truck and gate lift to me so I could pick up the bagels at the factory myself. Two, he suggested that I talk with their competitor about procuring product from them instead. At the end of the meeting, those were the two options on the table.

Picking up racks of bagels twice a week was not a viable or sustainable option, so it was a nonstarter. That would amount to picking up around twelve thousand to fourteen thousand bagels each week. Next, I approached the competitor. Their curiosity was piqued, and they asked a lot of questions. I relayed the information that had been given to me. They wanted our business, but their prices were too high. Getting product from them would also be more labor intensive. This was because their product came frozen in boxes. I would need to unbox the bagels, board them, rack them, and then thaw them, as we did not have an industrial freezer. This would mean hours of extra work every week.

I went back to our original supplier and just offered to pay more in order to continue our vendor relationship with them. He quickly presented a 20% price increase. I was of course more than happy to agree to the new terms. I wish he had just been upfront about wanting to implement a price increase from the beginning. There was no need to play games or make me jump through hoops. It would have been perfectly acceptable to me had that been presented from the start. I wouldn't even have tried to negotiate. I think he went about it in a roundabout way to show me the value of what he was offering and that the steep price increase would still be worth it.

The positive outcome was that I opened a new line of communication with a second bagel supplier. I started to buy some flavors from the competitor that the original supplier no longer offered. More variety of flavors was a win for me and our customers. Everything worked out well after that episode.

LABOR SHORTAGE

I didn't experience the labor crisis to the same extent. The biggest challenge was that our baker, a full-time staff member who had been with the Bagel Store since I started running it, tendered his resignation. Like many others during this period, there was surge in job mobility between job seekers and employers, resembling a game of tag. After a stagnant year, like most people, he also experienced the restlessness to seek better and higher-paying job opportunities. He found a more lucrative job in a company that manufactured and sold beds. I didn't begrudge his decision. I gave him my best wishes. I understood that he had to make the best decision for himself and put himself first.

A year or so later, he came back to work in the Bagel Store part time, baking and doing kitchen prep on Saturdays. I was incredibly lucky to work with the same person for so many years. It provided me with a sense of continuity and security, knowing that there were people in the store who had my back.

BAKING PARS

A baking par list outlines the number of units of each item that the baker needs to produce on a specific day of the week. It is important to strike the right balance, as the list constitutes a prediction of how many units can be sold on a particular day. Make too little, and the bakery might run out of stock early in the day, which will inhibit sales value. Make too many, and end up with too many unsold items at the end of the day, which will inflate cost of goods and translate into product waste. We were able to sell unsold bagels on the next business day, but at a heavy discount. We were also able to use them to make toasted sandwiches on the next business day, as the taste was still the same. I also donated the unsold bagels to the local food bank. Given everything, the bake list has a direct impact on both sales and cost of goods, so I cannot stress its importance enough.

The baking par list is also a living document that must continuously be modified from month to month or season to season, as the business normally sees fluctuations during the year or from year to year. Each day of the week has a different bake list based on past performance or forecasted sales trend. Different seasons and times of the year also dictate how many items we can sell. Lastly, the general trajectory of the baking pars list goes up as the business grows and evolves over time.

For the whole time I operated the Bagel Store, I had always been the morning baker—every day or most days. This meant I was intimately familiar with the sales trends and changes in demand. If there were a lot of leftovers from the previous day, I might bake a little less so we could still use the unsold bagels. If the previous day sold out, I might bake a little more to compensate. Like my management style, I fine-tuned, recalibrated, and had my pulse on the bake. It was all about striking a balance.

I can't believe I had a perfect attendance record in all of my years at the Bagel Store. The only time I was ever late was on my first week in 2015 when I was still training under the previous owner. Luckily, he was there to bake the bagels so the store still managed to open on time.

Other than that one instance, I was always able to open our doors on time with fresh bagels ready. I was never absent for a shift when I was scheduled. It was proof that the mind was more powerful than the body. I didn't give myself permission to get sick so it never happened. I started to feel it in the last few months though. I felt my body might possibly give out soon.

WAITING TIME

It's advantageous to become as intimately familiar as possible with the trends and flows of the business, industry, and market you are in. For example, our business was slower on weekdays. With a smaller staff on the roster, they needed to be all-rounders who were able to do a little bit of everything. I looked at weekdays as the days to pay the bills, whereas weekends were the days to make money.

The Bagel Store's sales grew until we eventually needed to staff eight people on weekends. One person took the orders. Three people were on the sandwich board: a slicer, a spreader, and a runner to take out orders. One person was the cashier. One person was the barista. One person was a floater—an extra person to answer the phone, wash the dishes, take out the trash, or take over any role if someone was pulled from the lineup to take their break. The last person was a dedicated kitchen worker who would prep for the next day so we wouldn't run out of goods.

Having a great workflow is a wonderful and exhilarating feeling. After enough time together, people develop a rapport and work as one. Everything seems to happen automatically and organically, as dependable as clockwork. A well-polished, synchronized way of doing things develops, with little to no need for verbal instructions. It makes such a big difference to have an experienced team who are used to working together.

It allows for a very smooth operation, like a symphony or lightning in a bottle. Everyone just has fun coming to work and takes things lightly. My favorite thing is just hearing people laugh the whole day when I'm in the back kitchen.

There are nuances in business that only an experienced manager is aware of. There were roles that were more important or that required a more experienced hand. Usually, we tasked new employees with being the order taker or the runner, which were seemingly the easiest and simplest roles on a weekend team.

However, this rationale would flip if we happened to be understaffed or if there was an unusual and unexpected rush of customers. When this happened, the order taker became the most important role in order to facilitate a smooth customer flow and experience. They were able to control the flow by intentionally taking their time talking to customers or asking them questions. In this way, they were able to slow down incoming orders and give staff working on the sandwich board, the cashier, and the barista time to catch up on existing orders on the board. I advised them to maintain a calm, slow demeanor and to essentially "play dumb." The order taker could also slice the bagels and put them in the toaster in between orders, as well as keeping an eye out and helping at the other stations when there were no new orders to be taken.

It's okay to tell customers to hold on for a moment. In general, they don't mind waiting if they see the employees are busy. On the other hand, it becomes an issue if they see employees doing nothing while they are waiting. (I also had a sign that said we couldn't handle any new orders because we were so backed up. Thankfully, we never used it.)

In my experience, it's better to break up waiting times rather than having one long, continuous wait. If a customer waits five minutes for their order to be taken, five minutes to pay, and ten minutes for their food and drink to be served, they won't notice or mind as much. They are less likely to get impatient and complain than if they were to breeze through the ordering process and pay, then wait a solid block of twenty minutes for their food.

I always tell the food runners that they are the final quality control and last check to make sure orders going out are accurate and match the order ticket. It seems like common sense, but I have to remind them to make sure that they give the right order to the right customer. It's interesting how many times a customer will just take a bag if you look them in the eye, even if it is not their name being called. The runner has to either repeat the name before giving them the bag, or tell the customer what the order contains. Then the customer has to verbally confirm that it is theirs.

It is always better to take a little extra time to make sure an order is correct rather than rush and take a lot more time to fix the mistake later. Service recovery is a critical skill to develop. In my experience, most angry customers just want to be acknowledged. As a general rule, apologizing profusely and sincerely is a good policy to live by in customer service. It costs nothing to be nice and pays handsomely to know how to deescalate tense situations.

I remember many little things fondly from those years. Older regular customers who came in on a daily basis, then one day just stopped coming in. Babies I saw growing up over the course of nine years. Employees who worked in the Bagel Store in high school, left to go to college for four years, then came back to work with us again in a different stage of their life. Before the gate to the Park N Ride was closed, we would get some colorful visitors at the store. Interestingly, drug addicts always had a fondness for our salt bagel. True story.

I remembered watching the ceiling-to-floor windows from the inside of the store – of cars rolling by with the people they carried. Everyone was coming or going somewhere. From there, I saw the changes in the seasons, from the lush green of summer to the fiery colors of fall. Snow descended from the sky in a cadence in winter and nature reawakened in the spring with brightly colored blooms. I remembered time going backward or forward with Daylight Savings, and how I always experienced it because the time jump always occurred on my shift as the Sunday baker.

CHAPTER 12

2022

INFLATION WAS the defining issue of 2022 and the crescendo from the last year's supply and labor shortages. The Bagel Store had started to see diminishing profit margins towards the tail end of 2021. Because of this, I decided to implement a price increase at the top of the year.

We increased prices by 15% across the board, which was the biggest annual price increase we had ever implemented. Price increases take planning, and the right process needs to be followed. I finalized the prices for each individual item and modifier (like small, medium, and large). I then approximated the standard profit margin of each item. I manually updated the pdf files for the bagel and beverage menu boards. We had light menu boards, so it cost around $500 to have them changed at the sign shop. I updated the prices on the point of sale system, counter signs and price tags myself. I don't put prices on the website but it's crucial that the prices advertised in the store are updated and correct.

Once, I changed the menu board color to a muted olive green to match the color of our walls. It became a radioactive green when backlit, like the glowing nuclear waste on The Simpsons. At night, you could see it shining from far away like a beacon. I went back to the sign shop to have the background color changed to black the very next day.

It seemed like we couldn't make the amount of money we had made in previous years. The cost of goods kept rising and fluctuating wildly and uncontrollably. We were still turning a profit from month to month, but I would often think to myself: Is what I'm doing worth the amount of money I am making?

I deliberated with myself over the course of the year whether to implement a second price increase. It was a difficult decision to make. We had never had two price increases over the course of one calendar year. I struggled with it because I put myself in the shoes of the customer. Even if some or most customers don't notice it, I just didn't feel that it was fair to them. I don't know whether that way of thinking is justified or not. Fortunately, in my situation, it was a small business, and there were no shareholders to answer to. The buck stopped with me. In the end, I couldn't increase prices for a second time that year, and I ended up absorbing the cost of inflation.

I cannot quantify the positive impact of having stable pricing over the whole year has on customers. Now, there is a lot of talk in the news about fast-food chains adopting dynamic pricing, where prices would fluctuate depending on factors like time of day or how busy it gets. I am not an advocate of that strategy for this reason. In my opinion, it is incredibly short-sighted to impose that on your loyal customers.

I'm proud that we offered consistent product quality and customer service at a reasonable price. We met customers' expectations each time they walked into the Bagel Store. I like to think that this long-term play paid off in the year that followed.

MANAGEMENT

I am not a naturally social extrovert, so it is curious that I went into a profession that involves a great deal of daily human interaction and forming and maintaining relationships with suppliers, vendors, service providers, customers, employees, property managers, and others. Funnily enough, the thing I was most proud of—and one of my greatest strengths as a business owner—was my people skills.

Professionalism is of utmost importance in business. Consistency is vital in dealing with employees with regard to giving directions, corrective actions, and expectations (as well as accuracy and timeliness of the payroll). Building rapport takes time. Over time, non-verbal communication becomes easier, as long as employees know and adhere to the rules and standards that you set for the store.

The weekly schedule was another fantastic tool to manage people in an indirect manner. Work performance led to prime shifts. The most coveted were morning shifts, when the pace was brisk, the tips were generous, and the day went faster. An ideal work schedule was an incentive for staff to uphold employee expectations and quality standards. At the same time, there were other considerations or compromises to building the weekly schedule. Staff members who lived far away were prioritized to receive longer and earlier shifts. This was to make the commute worth their while and avoid traffic. Employee dynamics was another important consideration. Even with a small team, interpersonal relationships played an important role. People who did not get along were put on different shifts as much as possible. Everyone wants to have a pleasant work day, which parlays to a pleasant customer experience.

My management style has definitely evolved over the years. In the beginning, I was hands-on. I took on as many responsibilities I could manage and filled the gaps left by employees. Later on, I let the employees sink or swim on their own. I was no longer their backup or safety net. This worked better for me and for them. I found that the employees were more responsible and self-reliant than I initially thought. Employee turnover also became significantly lower over time. Most people prefer to manage themselves and do things their way, which is perfectly acceptable if it works within the framework of the business culture and environment. I only lost my temper once with an employee. Regardless of the reason, I always felt shame that I let my negative emotions take hold of me. I promised back then that it would not happen again. I am so proud that I kept that promise from the early years of the Bagel Store.

EMERGENCY PLANNING

We had troubleshooting and different plans in place for events such as blackouts, snow, excessive heat, and credit card processing problems from the merchant services provider.

In the beginning, your mindset is to find a way and make it work—whatever it takes. Later on, you are able to assess the level of risk and judge whether the reward justifies said risk. I once picked up an employee in a winter storm because they lived in a hilly, slippery area. Because I was in such a hurry at 6 a.m., I slipped and fell on black ice.

The bakery was particularly tricky to operate in snow conditions. When the baker arrived early in the morning, snow would typically not have fallen yet. When I finished baking at 7 a.m., I would look outside to see the streets covered in snow. I would finish making a product that had to be sold on that same day, but very few customers could come in when it was snowing. Eventually, after years, we came up with a system. We would check the weather forecast for winter storm warnings. Before the baker came in, we'd create a group text with the staff scheduled for that day and assess whether the employees could come in. We would open a little later in the day so we could determine, together as a team, whether the weather and road conditions were safe enough to travel.

Our town is particularly prone to blackouts. Most of the time, the cause is wind causing trees to knock down power lines; other times, animals are to blame, according to the electrical company's app.

Cuts from sharp knives and burns from ovens were common

safety hazards in the Bagel Store. We always had to have a first-aid kit with an assortment of bandages and burn gels ready. At worst, an employee can go to the hospital and file a worker's comp claim for a serious accident. I handled knives hundreds of thousands of times but I was lucky I never sliced myself. However, I had my fair share of burns from the oven.

INFLATION

Like the previous year, the Bagel Store seemed to be a microcosm of what was happening in the broader economy and even the stock market, which were both pointing in the same direction in 2022. Down. The stock market fell over 20% in 2022 year over year. The inflation rate was at 8% and consumer prices went up 9%. It was a mini recession. In a similar fashion, we didn't generate as much income as the year before. The Bagel Store's future seemed fraught with uncertainty.

Money was just not coming in as it should have, even with my diversified income streams from my business operations, passive income, and portfolio income. In my experience as an entrepreneur and investor, you have to trust in your vision, stay the course, and trudge through the dry spells. A rising tide lifts all ships, and when it rains, it pours.

CHAPTER 13

2023

THE MARKET REBOUNDED, and so did the Bagel Store. I increased prices by 10% at the top of the year, and no more after that. The store became busier than ever with volumes through the roof. More importantly, this boom in sales also parlayed to our most profitable year on record. Higher sales plus controlled costs equaled maximum profit. In my professional experience at least, it seemed that inflation had stabilized, and some costs of business may even have softened a little bit. This was a transformative year for business in more ways than one.

However, something shifted after Covid-19. With how busy the Bagel Store had become, there was also more firefighting than ever before. Things like machine breakdowns, inventory, staffing, and technical issues became more pronounced. It got a lot harder to get out of town and leave the store even for a week.

And so I made the decision to sell the Bagel Store after nine years of operation. There were a number of considerations that factored into the decision. I concluded that it was the right time to sell. In 2023, which was our last full year of operations, we achieved our highest revenue and profit ever. December 2023 was our highest sales month on record. The broader market seemed to have recovered from the economic effects of the pandemic in the span of a few years. I believed I could fetch a good price for the business with a healthy markup over what I paid for it in in 2015.

My personal situation had flourished because of the business. In my time as owner, I learned so much and surpassed the personal and professional goals I had set for myself. During these years at the Bagel Store, I also found my footing as an investor and became my own personal financial planner. I homed in on the investing strategy that worked for me. At this point, I could still earn some passive income. Not enough to offset my living expenses or keep my assets intact, but still. There were some pleasant surprises along the way, like some grant awards, financial support from the government, claim settlements, and financial windfalls from the business. The experience was immeasurable. I spent my thirties and a decade of my life in the Bagel Store. I turned forty and wanted a new experience. You only have one life to live.

There were also the analytical and fiscal considerations. I knew I wanted to sell at the start of the next year because of tax considerations. I would only earn the proceeds from selling the business, which would result in capital gains. I wouldn't accrue income taxes from a full year of operational income that might push me in a higher tax bracket. It was the perfect time to sell.

Selling the store made me feel the same way I felt when I left my job at the Gelato Shop. Both times, I did not have a tangible plan of where I would land. I only had a mist of an idea of what would come next. I am pragmatic in the sense that I don't believe a person can have everything. Something has to give. You have to give up something in order to get something new. It's a matter of priority and choice. You need to make space to be able to work toward and achieve another goal. One door has to close for another one to open.

LOCATION

The Bagel Store was in a commercial center that was similar to a strip mall. When I first started, half of the spaces were vacant. Throughout the years, I saw the comings and goings of tenants and the fluctuation of the town center's capacity.

At one point, the property ownership conducted a major renovation, remodeling the exterior of the buildings to have a more modern appearance. The new design was more colorful and eye-catching. Each space had its own color, design, and style. On the downside, it was not as sturdy, well-insulated, and protected from the weather. The buildings were more exposed to the elements like heat or rain because of a smaller and shorter roof.

All things considered, the renovation process was not too disruptive to our business. By my approximation, we lost about 10% of business for the few months it took place. We obviously had no choice but to bear the noise, inconvenience, and parking shortage. We did get some additional business from the construction workers who worked on the project. They came in every day for their morning bagel and coffee fix. The renovation benefited the business in the long run, as the shop now had a more attractive facade. After the remodeling was complete, the landlord sold the commercial center to a new property owner. In hindsight, all of it was done to help fetch a higher price for the commercial property. Smart.

The biggest upset we experienced was during the early years of the pandemic, when only a few spaces in the center were leased and open for business. The commercial center went from half capacity to almost empty. But by and large, all of the spaces were leased again by 2023, the first time in eight years. The commercial center became bustling and busier than I had ever seen. This was a positive indication of the economy's recovery. A variety of new businesses moved in, like a martial arts studio, a ballet studio, a tutorial center, a chiropractor's office, a DMV office, and new cafés and restaurants, which brought new life and revitalized energy to the town center.

A standalone building near the Bagel Store was demolished to build a new Starbucks. A new café serving Korean desserts like bingsu and croffles also moved in several feet away from us. I was pleased that the new stores opened, as they contributed to more walk-in customers for the Bagel Store.

In my opinion, it is beneficial to have similar businesses near your location. It brought more customers to the area, and all the businesses benefited. There is a saturation point, however.

If there were more businesses than customers to serve, we would have faced a scarcity problem. Thankfully, our location was still unsaturated with cafés, sandwich shops, and bakeries, even after two new similar businesses came in.

I exercised both of my five-year lease renewal options for the Bagel Store: the first in 2018 and the second in 2023. That was another factor in the timing of the Bagel Store's sale. I wanted to give the eventual buyer at least four to five years on the lease before it expired. During that year's lease renewal, I had also negotiated an amendment with the landlord to add an additional five-year lease renewal option that would bring the owner to the year 2033.

SPECIAL PROJECTS

Besides the lease, I also set the table for the buyer (figuratively speaking). I completed two major projects that cost a total of almost $25,000, a considerable amount to be sure. The first project was to upgrade the store's HVAC unit from two tons to three tons. Mind you, the timeline and target closing date for the sale was in the winter. The buyer would have had no way of knowing that the HVAC wasn't sufficient to deal with extreme heat. This was only a problem during the summer on days with excessive heat warnings of over 90 degrees. The problem was that the HVAC unit was not meant for how the space was used: a food-service establishment with machines generating so much heat inside. Butter would melt to liquid if you left it out on a table. I remember that it would get unbearably hot depending on the year. Some years it would last for several days. Some years it would last weeks at a time.

The summer of 2021 was particularly rough. We had to put ice inside the sandwich fridge then.

We had a problem with the walk-in cooler one time. Our service tech got run over by a car and could not physically go up to the roof to diagnose the condenser. He asked me to go up there to inspect it and report back to him. While on the roof, I saw how old and dilapidated our HVAC was compared to the other tenants' units.

So I bit the bullet and replaced it with a higher-capacity unit that would be able to sufficiently cool down the premises during heat waves. It cost so much because it was a major project. We had to obtain a permit from the city and rent a crane to lift the unit up onto the roof. Thankfully, I got some rent credit from the landlord to cushion the blow. Still, the bulk of the cost I paid out of the Bagel Store's coffers.

I felt it was the right thing to do. I didn't want the new owner to go through what I went through for so many years. Besides, one of the tenants leasing that space had to do it eventually. For some sentimental reason, I also just believed in giving back to the store I had benefited from so greatly over the past nine years.

The second project was to replace the evaporator of the Bagel Store's walk-in cooler with a made-to-order evaporator with a special coating on the copper coil. This had been a tricky, ongoing maintenance issue since I started at the store. The evaporator would break down more or less every couple of years. I didn't know it at the time, of course.

Once it stopped working, it would need to be replaced right

away. This was because the cold room would not be able to cool down sufficiently to hold perishables at the adequate temperature. All of the food inventory would spoil. The evaporator could be replaced in a day or two, but those that were readily and locally available to purchase did not have the special coating. The coils would corrode again after another couple of years. The hypothesis was that the yeast in the bagel dough corroded the coils, leading to a recurring cycle of replacements.

According to our service tech, the coils with the special coating would supposedly last four times as long, or approximately eight years. The complication was that it took several weeks to fabricate, customize, and ship. So it had to be ordered before the existing evaporator showed signs of problems. We would need to spend the money and replace the evaporator while it was still operational. That was another one of those moments where I wished I had bit the bullet way earlier so I could have saved the money I spent on that cycle of repairs. I could have also saved myself a lot of headaches in the long run, and some tens of thousands of dollars.

These were a couple such things no one told me about. I only wished I had done these lease improvements earlier so I could have benefited from them. It took years to learn and understand the particular nuances and quirks of my business. I was still learning in my last years, weeks, and even days.

Even though I would no longer be the owner, I knew these problems would arise in the future. My mindset was to handle those scenarios in the same way I would have handled them if I were not selling the shop. Although that had not been my experience as a buyer and my seller had hidden some things from me, I felt a strong obligation to set my buyer up for success. As a caveat, what made it doable was how well the store was doing financially. There was cash in the bank for these last projects.

TRADITIONS

One of my favorite things to do was to set up store decorations for fall and winter. Fall decorations would go up after Labor Day. We had pumpkins on customer tables and every surface of the store. Fall colored leaves lined the walls, windows and doors. Owls made of cloth were suspended from the ceilings like they were in mid-flight. Scarecrows and brightly colored flowers were placed thoughtfully where eyes can wander and catch them.

These would go down and winter decorations would go up after Thanksgiving. We had little pine trees on customer tables. Wreathes with garlands and ornaments adorned the walls, windows and doors. The owls were replaced by snowflakes like they were falling down from the sky. Toy penguins, polar bears, reindeer, Santas and nutcrackers were aplenty. Cozy red, green and gold were the prominent colors when you walked in the store from the outside cold.

Most years and when it was safe to socially gather, we had a holiday party for employees where they played games like White Elephant, made arts & crafts, and cooked food for a potluck. I couldn't take credit though because they organized the event themselves. I loved giving Christmas gifts to the team. I usually prepared gift boxes with chocolates, cookies, popcorn and fresh fruit. I also had advent calendars and Target gift cards. In order to be fair, the amounts on the cards were based on how many hours they worked for the given period.

We celebrated employee birthdays with balloons, birthday cards and cupcakes. The last few years, I also distributed quarterly bonuses in the form of gift cards to show my appreciation and express my gratitude. I have experienced in a previous job an employer who placed their customers first and foremost above their employees. I believe that an employer should take care of their employees who in turn take care of their customers.

For the most part, it was a wonderful work environment. It was everyone's effort that made our little space feel like a second home.

CHAPTER 14
2024

I KNEW THAT I WANTED to close at the top of the year for income tax considerations. I had a full year of income from the previous fiscal year's operations, as well as other income from a grant award and some funding. I expected most of my 2024 income to come from the proceeds of the business sale.

I had gone through the process of buying and selling businesses from both sides several times at this point. One option was to approach the second bagel supplier, who had expressed some interest in the business. However, it was risky. I don't believe they would have paid a decent price since they had their own business concept and model. I chose a reputable seller's broker with outstanding marketing knowledge and skills to assist with the sale. I knew that I didn't have the necessary skillset or personality to broker my own deal. I agreed to a whopping 7% broker's commission, as I believed it would be worth it if the broker could fetch a good price for the Bagel Store. Business brokers have a higher commission rate than real estate brokers because there's different kind of work involved in brokering a business.

I had one buyer on the table. The broker advised me not to self-screen interested or potential buyers like I had done in the past. According to the broker, the most important consideration was whether the prospective buyer had the funds to make the purchase. (I am smart enough to know that everyone wants to advance their own self-interests, and a broker's main motivation is their commission.) We had some interest the year before, but none had the proof of funds to secure the purchase.

I agreed to meet with the interested buyers, who were a husband and wife. The prevalent sense that I got was that they intended to be active owners. This is what I wanted for the Bagel Store. I wanted an owner who would be actively involved and invest their time and energy to continue the store's track record of success. This was ideal because I believe that a business of that size would not thrive long term or be profitable with an absentee owner. There are so many nuances and details that can easily make or break a small business. It's a slippery slope if you miss those small details. There is a fine line between profitability and loss. Hiring a full-time manager for a business the size of the Bagel Store would just eat away at the store's profits. By my approximation, the store would be close to breakeven with a full-time manager's salary. What would be the point of having the business if you don't make money and still have to deal with its headaches, even with a manager? Ultimately, the buck always stops with the owner.

The couple made an offer that was below the asking price. The offer was acceptable to me, but I followed the broker's advice to make a counteroffer. That's the psychology of a negotiation. You don't want to just accept the offer, or the buyer will suspect that you are hiding something. They accepted the counteroffer, and we proceeded to sign a purchase and sale agreement. It was going to be a cash sale. Everything was going smoothly so far.

The couple made the due diligence and feasibility period very, very easy for me as the seller. This should have been the time for them to get to know all aspects of the business, from employees to vendors to customers. This is when you remove the contingencies and verify information from the prospectus so you can make a sound and informed decision whether or not to purchase the business. But they only asked for a simple equipment inspection and bank statements, which were fast and easy. I wasn't sure if they were so trusting of me because I had made such a good impression, or if they were really confident in their abilities, or if they were serious buyers. In any case, I was stressed out because there was radio silence for the whole month of the due diligence and feasibility period.

I knew that the buyers had extensive business ownership experience, but not in food service. From what the broker told me, they were very successful entrepreneurs. This was evidenced by how easily they passed the landlord's requirements for the lease reassignment.

Notably, the landlord didn't even require me as seller to stay on as a guarantor on the lease. This showed their strong confidence in the buyer to honor the lease agreement and be a model tenant, based on the history, experience, and financials that the buyer presented to them.

Back when I bought my two businesses, the landlord in both instances required my respective sellers to remain as guarantors or take second position on the lease. If I defaulted, the landlord could go after the guarantors. The sellers didn't really have a choice but to accept their conditions. Otherwise, the lease could not have been transferred and the deal would not have closed. Because of my limited experience and financial records, the landlords of the Bagel Store and the French Bakery didn't have full faith in me to run a profitable business and pay rent. I agree that their initial assessment was accurate. However, I am proud to say that I made all of my rent payments in full in all of my years of business.

I also have to give credit to myself. The landlord of the Bagel Store asked if the new owners would continue using the same business model. I had proved that it was a viable business many years over. It even survived through a global pandemic.

The landlord and property manager delayed drafting the document for the lease reassignment for a few weeks. They only gave their verbal okay and go-ahead. I feel like it was an intentional tactic to make sure both parties were serious about the deal. It was finally approved. Papers were drawn up and things moved very fast after that. Within a matter of days, we closed digitally by signing all the closing documents online. It felt anticlimactic not having a physical closing with the traditional shaking of hands and congratulations.

THE BUSINESS OF HUMANS

At that point, the staff had not yet been notified about the change of ownership. Typically, this would have been done a week before closing, and it's what I would have done as a final check and review to make sure I had employees to actually run the business. However, this buyer did not require it, so I did not press that button yet. My personal style is to answer questions and not volunteer answers. Anything you say can be taken in any way and may even hurt your deal. Better be safe than sorry.

We agreed on a three-week training period, which was included in the closing documents. I think of myself as a conscientious and detail-oriented person, but I like to be concise and organized as well. You can't give too much information all at once, or it will just be lost. I put together a binder with all the information the new owners would need: vendors, utilities, marketing, human resources, repairs, maintenance, passwords, and contact information. I also like to think ahead. Thanks to my years of operating and owning the Bagel Store, I could foresee what business information needed to be passed along.

I understood that my role would be completely different from that point forward. I handed the reins to the new owners, and they made the decisions. I could only offer information and support if asked. I guided the owners, gave them training, and concentrated on key areas that I personally took care of for the business, like baking, inventory planning, and purchasing.

I let the other staff train them in other areas such as customer service, front-of-house duties, and back-kitchen prep. After all, I could only do so much by myself in three weeks. I didn't handle much of these responsibilities anymore, so I was more than confident that the staff could train the owners up to the standards and rules we had set for the store. We had consistently met customers' expectations, and the Bagel Store was positioned very favorably at that point in time.

One day, while the owners were training, business was particularly slower than usual. They got really frustrated, thinking that the store was overstaffed and that the employees had nothing to do. This is often the perception that people who have not worked in food service have. You're making an assumption based on a snapshot, a very small window of time, and then extrapolating it to be the general rule.

You can walk in a store for thirty minutes and see nothing going on. However, it could have been extremely busy before or after you got there. Similarly, the owners were making a snap judgment based on one day's worth of observation, but the business did not operate in a vacuum. In the real world, one day can be very different from the next. A single day is not a reflection of the whole business that has operated for many years. I have a general idea of daily, weekly, and seasonal trends to be sure, but even I can't predict the outcome of every single day.

If I were in the buyers' shoes, I would have treated the first few months as an experiment and observation period. Take notes. See what works and doesn't work. Gather a sufficient data set and oversee the business for two or three months before making sweeping changes. (This was more than doable for them, since they had deep pockets.)

As a manager, I recognize there are days to make money and days to pay the bills. For the Bagel Store, Tuesdays through Thursdays paid the bills. Fridays through Sundays were when we made our money. It was a marathon. Consistency is so important in maintaining positive relationships with employees. I never took back shifts once I assigned them, even if business was slow. We would simply make up for it on another day when it was busier than usual. Peaks and valleys. It is important to keep your word because trust is so hard to build. A big-picture view and a long game require long-term relationships with people.

If schedule changes like shift additions or subtractions needed to be made, I would adjust the next week's schedule before it was released. Consideration goes both ways. It is a way to implicitly communicate that I keep my word and you should keep yours.

The new owners decided to terminate a third of the staff based on a week of observation. Most businesses' biggest pain point is staffing, and here was a perfectly capable, trained, and tested group of employees. I believe the expression is throwing away the baby with the bathwater.

This is not how I would've handled it, if it were me. From experience, I know that when the old employer leaves, a number of employees will follow suit and leave shortly after. It's just human nature. Typically, the older legacy employees are the most likely to quit. These are the employees who worked with the employer for a long period of time. They are used to the old way of doing things. If the new way is different (which it almost always is), it is harder for them to adapt. They become dissatisfied. Then, some of the newer employees with potential will rise to take their place.

I would have just waited if I were the new owners of the Bagel Store. This way, I wouldn't have blood on my hands, and my relationships with the rest of the legacy employees who stayed behind would remain intact. There would be no bad blood with anyone. The new owners had made a substantial investment, and treading lightly would have been wise, especially with the human component.

You can't un-ring a bell. Eventually, the employees who were not fired tendered their resignations in solidarity with their peers. A big reason they liked working at the store was its healthy and positive work environment and the people they got to work with on a daily basis. Sometimes, people have to learn things the hard way.

Later on, I found out that it was the one owner's best friend who allegedly influenced their decision. The best friend owned a pizzeria. She was then hired by her best friend to manage the Bagel Store. She had very strong opinions on how the store should be run. According to her, I apparently did not do a good job of running it. She wanted to change everything, even the tip structure. I was just shocked at everything that came out of her mouth. But I was unfazed. I have met a lot of people like her; people who talk a big game and can convince others they can do everything. Can she back it up? I don't know.

Allegedly, she was the person who suggested to the owner to buy the Bagel Store. She certainly took her friend for a ride. I suspect they did not remain friends for long after that. With all due respect, it felt to me at the time like these people invited a crazy person in their house and handed her their keys to the car.

The owners also brought in a man as a new employee. We were training together when I asked him if he had known the owners for very long. He said they had just hired him to work in their construction company. However, there were no job openings at the time, so they asked him to work at the Bagel Store in the meantime. He had no food-service experience or idea what type of compensation he would be receiving. I thought it was very bizarre.

It didn't matter to me. The check had cleared. I had already planned on paying the employees' severance before they got fired and the rest quit. I increased it to one or two months of pay so they would have a cushion until they could find a new job.

I felt bad about how things ended and wished it were different. However, every one of the staff was highly capable and I was confident they would be all right in the future.

CHAPTER 15

POST-CLOSING

AN IDEA THAT RESONATES with me is that people often act on the fallacy that their future selves are incompetent. They need to do everything now, so they can't stop what they're doing—for example, leave their job—even if they are unhappy. I agree with making and setting aside money for the future, but to a degree. Taking breaks need to be normalized if you are in the fortunate position to do so. I have faith in my future self that he will be able to pick himself back up and get back on the train. I trust that he will have a bright and optimistic future. I believe that, with the benefit of my experience, he will be better than I am today.

Life is a series of pivots, and it doesn't end until it ends. Giving myself that space to pivot allows me to recalibrate, re-center, and have the freedom to make decisions, even if they come with a great deal of uncertainty. It is time to figure out my identity without the business as a crutch. It can't be my whole reason for being. It may be foolish, but I think things always have a way of working themselves out. They have in the past, so there's no reason to believe they won't in the future.

As for my own takeaways from life? At the end of the day, all the steps I took from 2011 to 2024 were in pursuit of something that I can be proud of. I think that is what everyone wants, whether in their professional career or personal life. That's really why I went into small business. Building and cultivating something that I could call my own was a very uplifting experience. Some seeds I planted grew. Some seeds I planted didn't. I don't know if I would want to do it all over again, but I'm happy with what I created, maintained, enjoyed, shared, and inevitably walked away from.

As for takeaways from small business? Routine and repetition. Focus on the bread and butter of the business, even if it is not the most exciting. New products contribute incrementally. If you're lucky, they might account for 5% of total sales. Running a business is the most fun when it is making money. A retail store has limited space, like real estate. You want to maximize the real estate you have with products that can sell. Under-promise, over-deliver and guarantee accuracy to ensure customer satisfaction.

WHEN STARTING SOMEWHERE NEW

Land softly when entering a new environment. It is nice for customers to think it's business as usual and remain unaware, as if nothing had changed – unless the business is unprofitable or has been run poorly, or if employees are disgruntled and customers are dissatisfied. Then it makes sense to start off with a bang and make grand, sweeping changes, like announcing a change of management or ownership for the better.

I have also seen new owners who land hard and still succeed. It is important to note, however, that these individuals would typically have been tried and tested in the same industry. They have a proven track record in a similar or comparable company. In such cases, I would even argue that the new owner might have a better understanding than the previous one, with the potential to drive the business forward more quickly and effectively.

The takeaway is that you truly don't know the other party until after the closing date and the business has exchanged hands. Every former business owner has to contend with this fact. They have to understand that after the business is sold, you have to separate your identity from it. Of course I want it to do well, but I also recognize that I no longer have control over it. It is now the owner's success or failure.

From the outside, the French Bakery seems to be prospering under my buyer's care. I'm very proud, even though I have nothing to do with the business anymore. We only communicate during the holidays to exchange a cordial and perfunctory holiday greeting. Time will tell with the Bagel Store.

When I tell people that I sold my business, I generally get two reactions. People who have not owned a business express apprehension and concern that I did not have a next move ready and worry that I might regret my decision. I understand their reaction. But an exit strategy is equally important as entering a new venture. You have to learn to walk away at the right time, when gains can be maximized. You don't want to be left holding the bag. In contrast, people who have owned a business have a very simple reaction: I get it. Congratulations and well done.

The saying goes, "The second best day in a person's life is the day they buy a boat; while the best day in their life is the day they sell it." I feel like maybe the same can be said for business.

ESTATE PLANNING

As time passed, it became clearer that having an estate plan was a necessity to protect the assets I cultivated over the years and make it as easy as possible for the beneficiary that I choose.

I formalized my estate planning portfolio with the help of an estate planning attorney. It included the summary of estate planning provisions, the living trust & auxiliary trust documents, last will & testament, durable power of attorney – financial & medical, health care directive, and final disposition authorization & instructions. The attorney assisted in filing my real estate property's quit claim deed with the county. I added my trustee to my bank and brokerage accounts.

The whole process was simple but I believe the benefits will be more than worthwhile. It will save my loved ones from a lot of needless complications in any event.

WHAT'S NEXT?

A lot of people have a long-term plan or end goal. Others don't have one in mind. But the important thing is just figuring out how to get from point A to B to C to D. Like most people, I just took one step at a time. I took the most logical step, or the one that was available to me, until I got to the here and now. It led me somewhere I didn't expect. I look back and it amazes me how I got from point A to point M (the thirteenth letter and halfway point in the alphabet).

After selling the Bagel Store, I decided to take a break. And like a lot of people who completely stop, I eventually grew restless. For a while, I trained and worked as an apprentice baker at the Japanese bakery that I passed up on in 2015. It was satisfying to take a peek and experience a little bit of what could have been. It was also reaffirming to find out that I made the right choice all those years ago.

I volunteered, traveled back home and to different states, met old and new friends, and had all the experiences I missed out on for so many years. In what was my last year of business, it became a year of firsts – bird watching, paddle boating, hiking, camping, board game and trivia nights, amusement parks and museums, and social groups like the Rotary Club.

I did acts of service. I fostered cats inspired by my friend, Jeff, who has a cream-colored cat named Tucker. He liked to think that Tucker is a successful business mogul, and maybe he is. I wouldn't be surprised if an orange cat secretly ruled the world. I inadvertently kidnapped my left neighbor's cat, Leo, when he accidentally got out. I narrowly came close to kidnapping my right neighbor's indoor-outdoor cat, Blaine. Those are stories for a different book however.

I mourned relatives and pets that passed this year. I confronted the trauma and core wounds that had built up over many years. I can't say it was successful, but it was a start. Deep breaths, clear thoughts. Control what you can, let go of what you cannot. I reflected on the past and pondered the future. Everything is open which is both a freeing and terrifying thought.

Back when I had a regular income and extra cash in the bank, I made three angel investments in start-ups and emerging private companies. Although I practiced my due diligence like I did with entrepreneurship, I don't know how they will turn out. It will be several years until I do. I am hopeful they will reach an inflection point and consequently, a liquidity event. If none of them make a return, then that would be the end of that particular journey. If they do, I'll continue on that path with the proceeds that I receive.

I know I have at least one more business in me, but it might take some years to take that plunge again. I liken it to ending a long-term relationship. You don't want to jump in again too soon. I might find a job and do something different. I don't know where I fit in, but I'm sure I will figure it out.

ACKNOWLEDGEMENTS

For a book about business, writing this over the course of several months has been a surprisingly tedious, emotional and rewarding experience. I am incredibly happy to accomplish it and realize this dream. I couldn't have done it without Perfecto and Marilyn. You both have been there for me my whole life. You gave me unconditional love and support. To have you as my parents, I am blessed.

To my mom's sister, Evangeline, who sadly passed right before I started writing this book. She became its catalyst. Life is short. There is only one of it. But if you're lucky, you might get two. According to Confucius, the second begins when we realize we only have one. With that, I am reminded.

To Carlos, Sarah, Zoe, Olga, Becca, Victor, Andrew, Jesse, Sofia and every one of the 180 employees I had in 9 years. I felt supported and learned from each one. No matter how big or small, you all played a part in this story. For that, I am fortunate.

To AJ, Hussein, Sean, Alan, Jun, Kim and others, you were ideal collaborators in business and excellent entrepreneurs in your own right. I am inspired. To all of my brilliant customers, your smiling faces made coming in to work every morning a joy and every day a present. For giving us your loyalty and trust over many years, I am humbled.

To Dominic, Claire, John and Ramona, I learned everything about small business from you and I applied it to my own. You changed the trajectory of my life. To have you as my mentors, I am grateful.

Lastly, this book was formed with the help of my book editor Susan Gaigher, book designer Wayne Kehoe, Doug Fordice who was a confidant in the writing process and Alex Konicke who was a resource in the publishing process.

ABOUT THE AUTHOR

Martin Tiongson resides in the breathtaking Pacific Northwest. Originally from Manila, Philippines, he moved to Florida for school. He moved to South Carolina for a job. He moved to Washington State for a business. Soon, it will be time to move again for something new. This is his first book.

Email: *martin_tiongson@hotmail.com*

LinkedIn: *linkedin.com/in/martintiongson/*

Instagram: *instagram.com/martintiongson/*

Facebook: *facebook.com/martintiongson/*

www.ingramcontent.com/pod-product-compliance
Lightning Source LLC
Chambersburg PA
CBHW070714130626
46553CB00005B/1986